About the Authors

Paul French is a writer and analyst specialising in China's consumption economy and markets. He is currently the Chief China Representative of independent research publisher Access Asia, based in Shanghai. He is the author of several books on China as well as the well-received *North Korea: The Paranoid Pensinsula* (Zed Books).

Sam Chambers is a freelance travel and transport writer based in the north-eastern Chinese port city of Dalian. Sam has been covering China's thirst for raw materials for the past decade. He writes for a variety of Asian and European titles and provides analysis on Chinese transport matters for a variety of firms, including JP Morgan and CNN.

OIL ON WATER

Tankers, Pirates
and the Rise of China

Paul French and Sam Chambers

Zed Books
London & New York

Oil on Water: Tankers, Pirates and the Rise of China was first published in 2010
by Zed Books Ltd, 7 Cynthia Street, London N1 9JF, UK and
Room 400, 175 Fifth Avenue, New York, NY 10010, USA

www.zedbooks.co.uk

Typeset in England by Free Range Book Design & Production
Cover designed by Rogue Four Design
Printed and bound in Great Britain by the MPG Books Group, King's Lynn
and Bodmin

Distributed in the USA exclusively by Palgrave Macmillan, a division of
St Martin's Press, LLC, 175 Fifth Avenue, New York, NY 10010, USA

A catalogue record for this book is available from the British Library
Library of Congress Cataloging in Publication Data available

ISBN 978 1 84813 468 3 hb
ISBN 978 1 84813 469 0 pb

Contents

Tables, Boxes and Figures

Tables

List of Tables, Boxes and Figures

Boxes

Figures

Terminology and Definitions

barrel – 42 US gallons (158.9873 litres or 34.9723 Imperial (UK) gallons).

barrels per day (bpd) – measurement used to describe the amount of crude oil (measured in barrels) produced or consumed by an entity in one day.

bunker fuel – fuel consumed by the engines of a ship.

compensated gross tonnage (cgt) – the cgt concept was first devised by shipbuilders in the 1970s to provide a more accurate measure of shipyard activity than could be achieved by the usual deadweight ton (dwt) measurement. It includes a calculation of dwt (see definition below) as well as the number of man hours, the use of materials and the amount of yard-hardware used in production.

container ship – a ship designed to handle containerised cargo.

deadweight ton (dwt) – the maximum weight (mass) of a ship when loaded up to its summer load line (or the Plimsoll Line) therefore providing the sum of the weights of the cargo, crew, fuel, passengers and stores.

deadweight ton (dwt) handling capacity – the displacement at any loaded condition minus the lightship weight. It includes the crew, passengers, cargo, fuel, water and stores.

gross and net tonnage (GT and NT) – gross tonnage is the basis on which manning rules and safety regulations are applied, and registration fees are calculated. Port fees are also often calculated on the basis of GT and NT. GT and NT are defined according to formulas which take account, among other things, of the volume of the vessel's enclosed spaces (GT) and the volume of its holds (NT).

long ton – 2,240 pounds or 1,016.0469088 kg.

metric tonne – a unit of mass equal to 1,000 kg (2,205 pounds).

nautical mile – 1,852 m, 1.852 km, 1.1508 miles or 6,076 feet.

very large crude carrier (VLCC) – oil tanker between 200,000 to 500,000 dwt.

Geographical Note

Economists and geographers often have different definitions of the world that can cause confusion. For the purposes of this book East Asia is defined as encompassing China, Taiwan, the Korean peninsula (North and South Korea), Mongolia and Japan. South East Asia is defined as including Burma, Brunei, Indonesia, Malaysia, the Philippines, Singapore and Thailand as well as the nations of Indochina (Vietnam, Cambodia, Laos), Papua New Guinea and Timor Leste. South Asia, despite being largely north of the equator, is defined as primarily the Indian subcontinent as well as Pakistan, Bangladesh, Sri Lanka, Nepal and Bhutan.

Abbreviations

AGIP	Azienda Generale Italiana Petroli
AOSC	Athabasca Oil Sands Corporation
ASEAN	Association of South East Asian Nations
ASG	Abu Sayyaf Group
BIMCO	Baltic and International Maritime Council
BP	British Petroleum
CCP	Chinese Communist Party
CNOOC	China National Offshore Oil Corporation
CNPC	China National Petroleum Corporation
COSCO	China Ocean Shipping (Group) Company
CPPE	China Petroleum Pipeline Engineering Corporation
CSC	Cambodian Shipping Corporation
DNV	Det Norske Veritas (Norway)
DPRK	Democratic People's Republic of Korea (North)
ECA	Emission Control Area
EFT&E	European Federation for Transport and Environment
EU	European Union
FoC	flag of convenience
GAM	*Gerakan Aceh Merdeka* (Free Aceh Movement)
HKSOA	Hong Kong Shipowners Association
ICS	International Chamber of Shipping
IEA	International Energy Agency
ILO	International Labour Organization
IMB	International Maritime Bureau
IMF	International Monetary Fund
IMO	International Maritime Organization

INTERTANKO	International Association of Independent Tanker Owners
IPCC	Intergovernmental Panel on Climate Change
IPIC	International Petroleum Investment Company (Saudi Arabia)
ISF	International Shipping Federation
ITF	International Transport Workers' Federation
JBIC	Japan Bank for International Cooperation
KOGAS	Korea Gas Corporation (South Korea)
LNG	liquefied natural gas
MARPOL	International Convention for the Prevention of Pollution from Ships
MEND	Movement for the Emancipation of the Niger Delta
MEPC	Marine Environment Protection Committee
MES	Mitsui Engineering and Shipbuilding
METI	Ministry of Economy, Trade and Industry (Japan)
MNLF	Moro National Liberation Front
MOGE	Myanmar Oil and Gas Enterprise (Burma)
MSCHOA	Maritime Security Center – Horn of Africa
MSDF	Maritime Self-Defense Force (Japan)
NATO	North Atlantic Treaty Organization
NDRC	National Development and Reform Commission (China)
NGO	non-governmental organisation
NITC	National Iranian Tanker Company
NTM	Network for Transport and the Environment (Sweden)
NYK	Nippon Yusen Kaisha
OPEC	Organization of the Petroleum Exporting Countries
PDVSA	Petróleos de Venezuela SA
PRC	People's Republic of China
PRD	Pearl River Delta
RINA	Registro Italiano Navale (Italy)
RMB	Renminbi (China's unit of currency)
ROC	Republic of China (Taiwan)
ROK	Republic of Korea (South)

SCCT	Suez Canal Container Terminal
SCO	Shanghai Co-operation Organization
SECA	Sulphur Emission Control Area
SINOPEC	China Petroleum and Chemical Corporation
SLOC	sea lane of communication
SOLAS	International Convention for the Safety of Life at Sea
STCW	Standards of Training, Certification and Watchkeeping
TAPS	Trans-Alaska Pipeline System
UAE	United Arab Emirates
UN	United Nations
UNCLOS	United Nations Convention on the Law of the Sea
UNFCCC	United Nations Framework Convention on Climate Change
VLCC	very large crude carrier
WFP	World Food Programme
WTO	World Trade Organization
WWF	World Wildlife Fund
YRD	Yangtze River Delta

Acknowledgements

Sam Chambers would like to thank the many ship owners who have given him his ongoing decade-long crash course in shipping. A special thank you goes to Captain Charles Vanderperre, who passed away aged eighty-seven in September 2009. It was onboard his giant tanker, *Shinyo Ocean*, in October 2008 with Paul French that the genesis for this book was formed. When he started out reporting on this sector in 2000, Sam had no idea just how vast, vital and complex it is. He still marvels at its scale and innovation every day.

For colourful slices of American history he is indebted to both Edward Nilges and Barry O'Rorke. When stumped on China's oil port plans, Sam was able to turn to the able researchers at Flynn Consulting while other key research throughout the book was carried out by his colleague in Dalian, Katharine Si.

As a freelance journalist, Sam is always grateful to the many editors who continue to provide interesting assignments and feedback on articles written. Top of the list in this department is Bob Jaques, in charge of *Seatrade* magazine and an editor *non pareil*. Similarly, the folk at PSA International in Singapore have been generous to a fault in allowing Sam to write on many key topics discussed in this book.

Paul French would like to thank those analysts, economists and strategists around the world who have been giving of their time in discussing the rise of China and East Asia in the last two decades. The opportunity to spend most days watching Shanghai's development at first hand has been a marvellous education in emerging market economics and globalisation red in tooth and claw.

For the initial opportunity to write about pirates and piracy he is indebted to the *Asia Literary Review*. The introduction to chapter 1 'Life Without Oil' and chapter 5 'Piracy: The Nebulous Threat' first appeared as part of a longer article – 'Aye, There be Pirates!' – in the *Asia Literary Review*, Vol. 11, Spring 2009. Many thanks to the editor Chris Wood for permission to partially reprint.

It is also important to thank those that have allowed for the development of ideas that have fed into this book, especially Toby Webb and his team at Ethical Corporation in London and Matthew Crabbe of Access Asia in Kuala Lumpur.

The authors would both like to thank Tamsine O'Riordan and all the team at Zed Books in London for supporting and encouraging this project.

Oil on Water

Friday 3 October 2008 – The Bund, Shanghai

Shanghai is a city that wants it all. The city government has a list of goals and it's ticking them off one by one. Some are the sort of ambitions big cities in developing countries always have these days – more skyscrapers, a bigger airport, new shopping malls. But Shanghai aims higher than most. Shanghai wants to be an international city and the local planners are working towards it becoming a centre for knowledge workers, a world financial centre to rival Frankfurt and Hong Kong if not perhaps London and New York, as well as becoming Asia's largest shipping, distribution and logistics hub. It has a good chance of achieving all these daring goals within the next decade.

But there's one thing it seems the city authorities are not daring enough to do: leave on the lights that illuminate the world-famous riverside Bund past about 9 p.m. Because, while Shanghai is not short of ambition and, some might say, hubris, it is forced to try to conserve energy. Keeping on the lights along the riverfront late at night just isn't that high on the city's long list of power priorities.

The authors of this book have sat and watched the lights go out on Shanghai's Bund many times. We've spent many years living in the epicentre of the Asian economic miracle and we've been visiting the factories, shipyards, steelworks and power plants around China that have done so much to create this miracle. Everywhere we've heard the same story – energy is something to be conserved, valued and not wasted because there is often never quite enough of it to keep up with the expansion of the economy.

China is not alone. We've witnessed executives at Taiwanese plastics factories panicking that their oil reserves are dangerously low and similar examples all across Asia as the region has become the workshop of the world. What has become apparent is that two things are happening, largely out of sight. First, every day an increasing number of oil tankers are sailing towards East Asia bringing in the essential supplies of oil the region needs and, second, this process is fundamentally changing the way the oil business works, thinks and operates – from Arab oil-producing nations to new suppliers in Africa and Latin America, from the crews and owners of the world's fleet of oil tankers to the way governments react to anything related to procuring oil or that might possibly interrupt its smooth delivery.

So we decided to accompany 180,000 tonnes of crude oil from its starting point in the United Arab Emirates to Taiwan – just over 4,000 miles – to try to understand the economics of moving oil from its heartland to the region of the world that is now demanding it most vociferously. Tonight the lights along Shanghai's Bund will probably be on again – until about 9 p.m. – and tomorrow the factories, shipyards, steelworks and power plants of East Asia will all be busy. That 180,000 tonnes of crude oil made the voyage is part of the reason why this is happening but it is also part of the reason that that process is so fragile. The voyage we undertook in late 2008 is, quite simply, the most important voyage any ship is making right now to keep the world economy turning.

The statistics are staggering: annually oil tankers collect, transport and deliver approximately 2,000,000,000,000 metric tonnes – over two-thirds of the world's crude oil supply. Globally over 87 mn barrels of oil per day (bpd) are produced, mostly in the Middle East and across the Russian Federation and the territory of the former Soviet Union, but reserves are found and exploited on every continent. Production is growing and the bulk of the increase is coming from non-member states of the Organization of the Petroleum Exporting Countries (OPEC),[1] who now comprise 65 per cent of total world production. Globally approximately 80 mn bpd are consumed, overwhelmingly in North America and Western Europe but increasingly in the emerging economies of China, the rest of East Asia, South East Asia and the Indian subcontinent. North America and Western Europe remain the regions most heavily reliant on oil imports. However, it is in East Asia, South East Asia and India that import levels are growing fastest and where dependency on imported oil, with the vast bulk arriving by sea, is becoming a relatively new cause of intense concern to the region's governments, military commands and corporations.

As countries develop, industrialise and urbanise so invariably living standards rise, driving up energy use overall, most often of oil. The prime example of this phenomenon currently is China, where oil consumption has grown by 8 per cent annually since 2002, doubling in the decade between 1996 and 2006. China's factories consume large amounts of oil but its burgeoning urbanised consumer society is also glugging oil at rapidly increasing rates as Chinese families become car owners, switch on their newly purchased appliances and begin to travel on holiday and for business in planes. India is also urbanising and industrialising fast – oil imports to India are expected to more than triple from 2005 levels by 2020, rising to 5 mn bpd from the current 2.9 mn bpd, chasing China, which now consumes close to 8 mn bpd.[2]

And the demand for oil will continue to grow. Consider just one statistic from one country (admittedly a statistic that has serious ramifications for oil use from a vast and populous country): at present China has approximately one-twentieth as many cars per person as the United States (35 mn cars for 1.3 bn Chinese as opposed to 185 mn cars for 300 mn Americans) but the gap is closing fast – in 2008 car sales totalled 9.38 mn units in China, now the world's second largest car market after the US and projected to grow another 5 per cent in 2009.[3] The McKinsey Global Institute estimates that China will have about 120 mn cars on its roads by 2020.[4] Even China's newly introduced fuel efficiency standards for cars and other measures, such as restrictions on car use in Beijing and other large cities, will mean the demand for petrol will continue to grow apace.

Like it or not, oil is a bedrock of economic progress globally and nowhere more so than where manufacturing industry is most heavily concentrated and expanding – again that is currently in the East, South and South East Asian regions as the West becomes increasingly service-industry oriented and outsources production and manufacturing to Asia. Oil is also the foundation of consumer society, allowing products to be manufactured and purchased, cars to be driven, planes to fly and lights and appliances to be switched on. East Asia, particularly China, is where a new consumer society is growing fastest, where urbanisation is occurring most rapidly – developments that currently affect most people on the planet. Alternative and renewable energies are becoming more advanced and more commonplace, with national governments investing more in their development and application (not least East Asian governments keen to limit both their environmental degradation and imported oil dependency), yet the fact is that oil will remain central to economic growth, industrialisation and urbanisation for the foreseeable future.

As the vast bulk of the world's oil is moved across the oceans in tankers, the transportation of oil on water is a crucial global issue affecting every nation, business and individual. However, despite its acute importance, the various issues surrounding the movement of oil on water, from piracy to ship ownership and working conditions onboard tankers to ship safety, have been conspicuously absent from the mainstream press and left to the specialist energy and shipping media. The exception is when a spectacular event occurs, such as a vessel being kidnapped off Somalia or a wrecked ship spilling oil onto Australia's Queensland beaches (as occurred in March 2009 when the container ship *MV Pacific Adventurer* spilled 230 tonnes of fuel oil, 30 tonnes of other fuel, 31 shipping containers, and 620 tonnes of ammonium nitrate into the Coral Sea during Cyclone Hamish). Then the media and the public sit up and take notice, though rarely, if ever, are the underlying issues and ramifications of the movement of most of the world's oil across the sea discussed in any depth.

Moving oil across the oceans is a key component of international 'energy security'. Most people are now quite familiar with the term but its meaning has changed somewhat since it first became common parlance in the 1970s. Originally 'energy security' referred mainly to confrontations in oil-producing states that threatened supply at the point of extraction, primarily in relation to the 'Middle East' (but also the Angolan Civil War, the Iranian Revolution and other events of the time) and its myriad problems and tensions. However (the Gulf War of 1990–1991 and the invasion of Iraq in 2003 notwithstanding), by and large confrontations in energy markets have given way to multilateral dialogue and formally composed structures that facilitate negotiation

4

rather than confrontation between states. At the same time, energy supplies have become more diversified, more transparent, with improved pricing regulation. Energy supplies from outside the Middle East have steadily increased everywhere: from Africa and Latin America to the entry of the former East European Bloc and the former USSR into the world oil market after the end of the Cold War and the rise of the new 'petrodollar' economies of Russia and the Central Asian republics.

Any interruption to the smooth flow of oil supplies by tanker across the seas is now a major threat to the economies of both producer and consumer nations – the issue of piracy around the Horn of Africa alone and the rapid reaction of a multilateral naval force to counter it indicates that controlling and protecting the movement of oil is now as crucial to nation states and multinational bodies such as the North Atlantic Treaty Organization (NATO) and the European Union (EU) as safeguarding the points of oil extraction. It is certainly true that oil price shocks have impacted dramatically on the economic performance of major importing countries. Repetitions of the events of the 1970s such as the Arab oil embargoes (1967; 1973–1974) and the Iranian Revolution (1979) still have the ability to generate recessions, spiralling inflation rates and severely curtailing economic growth in countries dependent on oil imports. Nevertheless, today the focus of energy security is increasingly focused on the ability to guarantee that all-important uninterrupted supply of oil from producer to consumer.

There is a stark imbalance between supply and demand in the global oil business. Simply put, those nations that require the most oil have only limited domestic reserves. This has been the case since World War II and the withdrawal of the European colonial powers from the major oil-producing countries of the Middle East and the subsequent independence of those countries. But this imbalance is now being further and significantly enhanced by East Asia's economic rise and in particular the rapid economic growth of China. To a lesser extent, this also applies to India, a vast and populous region with limited domestic oil reserves and a growing dependency on imports to sustain growth. As the global weight of demand for oil shifts evermore eastwards so this resource gap is becoming more pronounced.

Japan has no significant domestic oil or gas fields whatsoever and is forced to import in excess of 95 per cent of its oil requirements, with the overwhelming majority having to be brought to the Japanese islands by sea. Taiwan and South Korea are similarly vulnerable with low domestic deposits but growing manufacturing economies and urban conurbations demanding more oil. The island of Taiwan is reliant on tankers crossing the South China Sea and entering the contested Taiwan Straits for 98 per cent of its oil supplies while South Korea is a virtual island with sea on three sides and the impenetrable, intransigent and unpredictable Democratic People's Republic of Korea (DPRK) cutting it off from overland pipeline supplies via China or the provinces of the Russian Far East. Consequently South Korea is forced to import over 97 per cent of its oil requirements entirely by sea.

Even those South East Asian nations to the south with previously relatively large domestic reserves have found their economic growth outstripping their supply, forcing them to become oil importers. Malaysia and Vietnam were traditionally significant oil exporters even after fuelling their own domestic economies. Vietnam remains a net crude oil exporter, but finds it necessary to import refined oil due to a lack of refinery facilities. In January 2008 the country became a net oil importer for the first time in order to support its continued economic growth. Malaysia's major oil producer, Petronas (Petroliam Nasional Berhad), has warned that Malaysia will probably become a net oil importer in 2010. Vietnam has already seen that moving from being a net exporter to a net importer leads to a growing national deficit and current account gap, while any downturn in the profitability of Petronas (which is wholly owned by the Kuala Lumpur government) will have important ramifications for Malaysia. The other major economy in South East Asia in terms of population and landmass, Indonesia, became a net importer of oil in 2004. It should also be noted that the two smaller, but important, trading-dependent economies and major container ports in the region – Hong Kong and Singapore – are both entirely dependent on oil imports.

Even with the global economic slowdown in late 2008 and 2009 China's continued industrialisation and urbanisation ensured that it continued to import additional supplies of oil. In July 2009 alone China imported 119.3 mn barrels of crude oil via ocean-going tankers, approximately 26 per cent more than in July 2008,

6

according to China's Ministry of Transport in Beijing. This was a new monthly record for the country's total crude oil imports, exceeding the previous largest monthly shipment – 126.8 mn barrels imported in March 2008, a figure that included rail and pipeline supplies as well as seaborne. To understand China's true capacity to guzzle oil, domestically produced oil and that arriving via rail and pipeline from Central Asia would have to be added to the seaborne tanker-delivered supplies. In January 2009 China's dependence on imported foreign oil reached 50 per cent for first time.

And now the growing dependence of the rising East and South East Asian economies on imported oil is increasingly being matched by South Asia with the concomitant rise of India. India's growth has lagged behind China's somewhat in gross domestic product (GDP) terms and the country's developers have been slower to build infrastructure, as have its consumers to buy cars (the desire for ownership of cars in both countries is massive), but, like China, it has been rapidly urbanising and increasing its energy needs. India does have some oil reserves and is attempting to develop more, such as the Rajasthan oil fields.[5] However, India is producing only around 800,000 bpd, which may rise to approximately 950,000 bpd by 2011, but is consuming approximately three million barrels a day and so having to import between 75 and 80 per cent of its requirements while India's refiners are dependent on imported crude. Currently, India consumes far less oil per day than China but also has less domestic reserves and production facilities and so has to rely on importing a greater percentage than China.

East Asia's economic future is increasingly tied to oil supplies, and crude oil imports from outside the region now have to supply over two-thirds of East Asia's total consumption. For countries such as Taiwan and Japan imports account for virtually all their requirements, while rapidly developing and industrialising economies such as China and India rely on imported oil for between one-half and two-thirds of their required supplies. These dependency ratios will only grow – neither China nor India has significant untapped oil reserves to call upon; their economic growth (even if dampened by the economic slowdown in 2008–2009) will continue vastly to outstrip their ability to increase domestic oil production. Importing the bulk of their energy requirements is now a fact of daily economic life for the world's two most populous and rapidly urbanising nations.

Though the bulk of oil imported globally comes from the Middle East, wherever, whenever and however any short-run supply interruptions occur – political instability in supplier countries or pirates disrupting sea lanes – East Asia in particular faces a huge risk. China and India, as well as to a lesser extent the other nations of East Asia, have a more pressing need to be involved in protecting global sea lanes and preventing political conflict in supplier countries and regions, and are being forced to adopt an increasingly non-traditional partisan and engaged stance diplomatically, commercially and militarily when it comes to ensuring the constant flow of oil.

This is the reality of oil supply at the end of the first decade of the twenty-first century – it is still overwhelmingly moved from supplier to consumer by sea in large tanker vessels and will continue to be seaborne for the foreseeable future. Any threat to that transportation process becomes a serious threat to national development and the wider East Asian and Indian economy. For this vast and populous region to continue to rise economically and improve its collective standard of living, for the greater globalisation project that increasingly relies on the rise of Asia, the continued economic success and living standards of the developed Western economies and the continued stability and wealth of the producer nations across the globe, the security of the sea lanes and the organisation of efficient transportation of oil are vital issues too often left to a relatively small and specialist community to consider and discuss. This book intends to bring the issue to a wider audience.

The following chapters look at the issues around the rising consumption of oil and its transportation globally on every continent. However, there is a particular focus throughout on the phenomenal rise of East Asia, and particularly the People's Republic of China (PRC), because its role as an oil consumer in the last two decades has led to a massive and highly significant shift in the demand for oil globally and in where larger amounts of oil are being shipped or piped to. As the manufacturing economies of East Asia – China, as well as Taiwan, South Korea, Japan and South East Asia – have grown so has the demand for oil to fuel these economies, bringing a major shift East in global oil economics (chapter 1, 'Life Without Oil').

8

Importantly, significantly less well understood is that this shift East is also occurring in terms of who is investing in whose petro-facilities and economies, who owns the world's oil tanker fleet in charge of moving the bulk of the world's oil and who is crewing those tankers. All of these aspects have undergone rapid change – it is East Asians who are now investing heavily in the petro economies globally, particularly the newly emerging ones in Russia, Africa and Latin America. The points of supply as well as the destinations of oil are diversifying and proliferating (chapter 2, 'The Shift East').

Between 2004 and 2008 China accounted for fully 40 per cent of the total increase in world oil consumption, surpassing Japan to become the second largest gas-guzzling nation in total terms after the United States. This has had serious ramifications for the oil-producing states of the Middle East as well as other producer states across the world, large and small – from Central Asia to Africa to Latin America. China has become a major consumer, seemingly immune to price fluctuations in per barrel costs and ever hungrier. The reason is simple – China's growth and development, as well as ultimately the security of its Communist Party state regime, rely on an expanding economy, and that expanding economy requires oil – ever larger gulps of it. China's demand, as well as that of the greater East Asian region and India, is being further boosted by its rapid urbanisation and growing consumer wealth (chapter 3, 'The Great Voyage').

The second aim of this book is to deal with the raft of political, social and business issues that have emerged in the twenty-first century to threaten the smooth operation of the global transportation of oil. As noted above, most of the problems around the movement of oil on the ocean to ensure supplies are ultimately about ensuring the security of the world's sea lanes of communication (SLOCs, chapter 4 – 'Securing the SLOCs'), a term used to describe the primary maritime routes between ports. Some of the problems afflicting the smooth operation of the world's SLOCs do sound rather old – the resurgence and serious escalation of piracy, for instance, which has lately captured headlines around the Horn of Africa off the coast of Somalia. The rise of piracy represents a major threat to the unencumbered and safe operation of the world's SLOCs and may also be inspiring a resurgence of piracy in other parts of the world, from the Malacca Straits to Brazil (chapter 5,

'Piracy: The Nebulous Threat'). Others factors are distinctly less often reported, such as the problems affecting the men and women who crew the world's tankers currently in service (chapter 6, 'The Criminalisation of Crews'). Added to this is the question of ship ownership and safety, including the longstanding flag of convenience (FoC) arrangement (used by more than half of the world's merchant ship fleet), which is primarily aimed at reducing operating costs or avoiding government regulations, and can make the enforcement of law at sea problematic (chapter 7, 'Flags of Convenience').

If oil tankers are here to stay then there are questions about their impact on the environment. Shipping has attracted less press and pressure group attention than air or road transportation, but there are issues to be considered and there is a clear environmental impact to moving 2,000,000,000,000 tonnes of oil a year by sea that necessitates some sort of response and concerted action on the part of the world fleet's owners (chapter 8, 'Green Shipping?').

Finally, while sea transportation will continue to be the major method by which oil is moved globally for the foreseeable future, land-based and undersea pipelines are also proliferating, with many more planned as oil consumer countries and economies seek to diversify and guarantee their oil supplies, and producer countries seek to maximise their delivery volumes and profits. At present, pipelines carry only a minor percentage of the oil delivered globally (though at some point virtually all oil travels partially through a pipeline) and are seen by most nation states as even more vulnerable to intra-national disputes, internal conflicts and terrorism. Nations seeking energy security need to diversify their supply lines and so pipelines remain an issue (chapter 9, 'The Politics of Pipelines').

This book is intended as an introduction and examination of the issues raised by the shifting and increasingly unbalanced relationship between oil producers and oil consumers, and particularly of the intermediate part of that relationship – the shipment and delivery of oil from one to the other. It is perhaps worth noting at this point that this book is not about the business of oil extraction, the setting of prices per barrel, the great and hotly disputed 'Peak Oil' debate,[6] the rise of alternatives to oil, renewables or the history and activities of the major oil companies, which are covered in many other books. The simple point of *Oil on Water* is to examine where and how much oil is moving around the planet on any given day, why its uninterrupted journey is important and the threats to that voyage.

CHAPTER ONE

Life Without Oil

Sunday 5 October 2008 – The Port of Singapore

The Shinyo Ocean *is carrying 180,000 tonnes of oil from Fujairah in the United Arab Emirates down the Malacca Straits, around Singapore and then up past the east coast of the Malay peninsula, Vietnam and across the South China Sea to the island of Taiwan. It's a regular route – owned by a European, the Hong Kong flagged very large crude carrier (VLCC) is contracted to make the run several times a year by Taiwan's plastics industry, which has a thirst for oil that requires constant quenching.*

The ship doesn't stop at Singapore, just slows down to pick us up along with some supplies and the essentials of shipboard life – newspapers and SingTel mobile phone top-up cards for the crew. Nobody buys anything else in Singapore – supplies for the run are taken on board in Fujairah – tax free – everything from cigarettes to booze to ice cream.

We head out just over an hour from Singapore's World Trade Centre Ferry Terminal to meet the Shinyo Ocean *aboard a small supply vessel, the* Jolly Rachel, *owned and crewed by three guys from Indonesia's Aceh province who lost their village to the tsunami and seem to have stayed at sea ever since. The tanker is late – caught in traffic, as the shipping lanes around Singapore are packed. Roughly 80 per cent of the world's seaborne freight and oil passes down Malaysia's coast, round Singapore and into the South China Sea or vice versa. We bob about for an hour starting to feel nauseous from the choppy sea and the endless shrill Indonesian pop music blasted at us courtesy of the* Jolly Rachel's *captain.*

The Shinyo Ocean *lives up to its 'very large' designation – 1,100 feet long, 200 feet wide and riding about 66 feet out of the water – basically a floating island fully loaded with oil and a twenty-two-man Indian crew. The ship is plenty big enough to allow you to go for a jog around the deck if the sea is calm. She's an expensive piece of floating real estate too – the ship alone is worth US$130 mn, while she's carrying a cargo of oil worth over US$120 mn and, in addition, she needs 62 tonnes of 'bunker fuel' a day to power the ship – at US$800 a tonne that means we're spending nearly US$50,000 a day just to keep moving. Factor in the additional costs of all the necessary lubricants, fresh water and food we need aboard and you start to understand how expensive it is to move the 'black gold' around the world.*

The captain slows to 7 knots to pick us up, dropping her side ladder as the supply boat comes alongside. At sea level with a VLCC tanker looming up 66 feet above you, 7 knots feels like a hundred; you jump the small gap and then climb up the sixty or so stairs to the deck with your head down, concentrating on putting one foot in front of the other. The Jolly Rachel *pulls away sharply as soon as we're aboard – even at these slowed speeds a small boat is fairly powerless against the* Shinyo Ocean *– if either captain isn't paying attention and lets the speed drop then the* Jolly Rachel *could get sucked as if by a magnet onto the side of the* Shinyo Ocean *and then pulled underneath it. If they weren't looking, the crew of the tanker wouldn't even notice the* Jolly Rachel *being pulverised. Once we're aboard, the captain can increase speed to 14 knots and by nightfall we're passing out of the Singapore Straits, into the South China Sea and close by the Riau Islands of Indonesia.*

It's six days constant sailing across the South China Sea to Taiwan.

The Imperative of Strategic Reserves

Oil tankers are the behemoths of the world's oceans and absolutely vital to the smooth running of the global production process. Email can go down for a few days, mobile phone signals be lost temporarily, pipeline supplies interrupted intermittently, but if oil tankers stopped sailing for a matter of days or weeks then the world's economy would literally grind to a halt.

The situation is potentially very serious – according to a March 2001 agreement, all twenty-eight members of the International Energy Agency (the IEA)[1] must have an inventory, or 'strategic petroleum reserve', equivalent to ninety days of the prior year's net oil imports for that country. Only a few net-exporter members of the IEA are exempt from the reserve requirement: Canada, Denmark, Norway and the UK. Recently even Denmark and the UK have both created strategic reserves to protect their economies from any interruption in supply.

Currently most nations are operating below the IEA-proposed ninety days – the United States current inventory of 724 mn barrels equates to just thirty-four days of oil at current daily US consumption levels (21 mn bpd). Japan's reserve would allow it to function for just over ninety days. In the EU the situation varies – usually between fifty to ninety days – while in Australia the strategic petroleum reserve equates to just ten days' supply.

However, the emerging powerhouse production economies of East Asia and India, which are the fastest-growing importers of oil, are on far shorter timelines and thus considerably more vulnerable to interrupted flows of delivery. South Korea and Taiwan have approximately thirty days of reserves but China has barely a fortnight's strategic reserve in stock, though it might last out thirty days if stocks held by enterprises are also factored in. India, similarly, has approximately a fortnight's reserves in hand.[2]

Any interruption to the world's SLOCs – whether it were war, internal conflict, piracy or industrial action that blocked any of the vital choke points between the Middle East and the major consuming markets to the West or East – would rapidly be a problem of global proportions. As more and more oil is moved east of the Middle East to East Asia any escalation of problems in the Straits of Hormuz, the Indian Ocean, the Malacca Straits, the Singapore Straits, the South China Sea or the Taiwan Straits could bring the world's new centres of production to a grinding halt. Consider that the Straits of Hormuz at their narrowest are just 33 miles wide, yet approximately 25 per cent of the world's oil supply and over 75 per cent of Japan's oil passes through them daily (something approximating a daily oil flow of 16.5–17 mn barrels or roughly two-fifths of all seaborne traded oil). The Malacca Straits – the crucial connecting passage between the Indian Ocean and the South China Sea – are barely 1.5 miles wide at their narrowest, yet a quarter of all oil carried by sea passes through them, mainly to the markets of East Asia. Vulnerability is the hallmark of the SLOCs.

Most people never see an oil tanker except on television on the relatively rare occasion when one gets into trouble. To most people Somali pirates with their automatic weapons and rocket-propelled grenade launchers are a distant and slightly baffling phenomenon. Little, if any, attention is paid to how many tankers sail the world's oceans, where they go, and who owns and crews them. That oil will arrive somehow, almost magically, and power our economies is taken for granted by most of us. It happens largely outside public view and public consciousness. Oil tankers do not attract the same fascination and media attention as other more visible forms of transportation and transmission of goods and ideas – roads, planes, telephones, the internet. And yet even a slight interruption to the smooth and uninterrupted global flow of oil from producers to consumers would have potentially devastating consequences for consuming nations – from unemployment and closed factories to blackouts and public health crises. Any prolonged interruption to the SLOCs and regular seaborne oil supplies could precipitate internal conflicts, civil strife and even war.

The oceans are the transportation method of the overwhelming majority of the world's oil – highways for the transmission of vital energy supplies – creating wealth for the producer nations and delivering ever larger doses of energy to consumer nations. Oil moves on water – if it ceases to, for even a short time, the world has a major problem.

Oil and the Getting of It

Oil is never far from the news. However, in recent decades the focus has overwhelmingly been on three factors: oil producers, oil consumers and the price of a barrel. This book argues that the missing part of the debate around oil for many commentators and the general public has been the transportation of this 'black gold' from producer to refiner to consumer. Moving oil, primarily by sea (which is the focus of this book), or by pipeline, involves discussion of a wide range of subjects. Invariably and in the case of the bulk of the world's oil, this movement involves transfer from one country to another and often from one continent to another. The ability to move oil successfully from A to B is of crucial concern to the producer nations, for without this they cannot trade and profit from their reserves. It is crucial to the consumer, whether a nation, a factory or an individual at the petrol pump, as without a secure and uninterrupted method of transportation demand would soon exceed supply in the countries with the heaviest usage, shortages would ensue, economies would start to slow and blackouts would follow. And, of course, the cost of transportation ultimately affects the final cost of oil to the consumer – the transportation of oil in whatever form it occurs must eventually be factored into the price paid at its destination.

Table 1.1 **Top fifteen countries with largest proven oil reserves, 2008**

Country	Reserves ('000 mn barrels)	Share of total global reserves (%)
Saudi Arabia	264.1	21.0
Iran	137.6	10.9
Iraq	115.0	9.1
Kuwait	101.5	8.1
Venezuela	99.4	7.9
United Arab Emirates	97.8	7.8
Russian Federation	79.0	6.3
Libya	43.7	3.5
Kazakhstan	39.8	3.2
Nigeria	36.2	2.9
USA	30.5	2.4
Canada	28.6	2.3
Qatar	27.3	2.2
China	15.5	1.2
Angola	13.5	1.1
Total World	**1,258.0**	**100.0**

Source: BP *Statistical Review of World Energy*, June 2009

While many are concerned about the very real fear of the depletion of the world's reserves of oil, the number of points at which oil is being sourced from around the world are actually growing. The now dead Cold War, which saw some major consuming nations unwilling to deal with some major producing nations and vice versa, led to the opening of new markets. Now that ensuring supply has become the crucial factor, pretty much everyone deals with everyone else. While the major world oil reserves may be declining (in 2006, a spokesman for the largest oil corporation in the world, Saudi Aramco, publicly admitted that its mature fields were now declining at a rate of 8 per cent per year[3]) new ones are found in places where serious exploration work is being done for the first time – in African nations such as Mauritania and as a result of various deep-water explorations and finds in the Gulf of Mexico for instance. The search goes on and in the last few years there has been a steady stream of new finds around the world.

Since the turn of the new century the Middle East's proven oil reserves have been revised upwards by 5 per cent (admittedly a matter of great and ongoing dispute), the former Soviet Union's by 35 per cent (as the country entered the world market and revealed more detailed data for the first time), while Africa's proven reserves rose by 45 per cent, as many previously unexplored and unsurveyed areas of the continent were examined and found to contain reserves. The new announcements of reserves have kept on coming in the last couple of years:

- In South America Petrobras, Brazil's national oil company, announced a new offshore field of between 5–8 bn barrels of recoverable light oil. In Mexico, an exploration well drilled near the offshore Ku Maloob Zaap heavy oil field, the country's most prolific producer, indicated that reserves at the complex could be greater than Mexico's state oil company Pemex had previously thought. The Gulf of Mexico is attracting much attention with a range of European, Asian, North American and other countries exploring, and now drilling, including those who would dearly love to raise their oil revenues, such as Cuba.
- In North America new finds are being made in the Gulf of Mexico as well as in North Dakota in addition to the highly contentious finds and potential further discoveries in Alaska and the Arctic.

- In Europe there have been new finds in the North Sea.
- In Africa, north of the Sahara, the Kuwait Energy Corporation recently announced two new oilfields in Egypt's East Ras Qattara block, which could boost production from 900 bpd to 5,285 bpd of light crude, while the Algerian state-owned energy group Sonatrach announced seven new hydrocarbon finds in 2009 alone. South of the Sahara, Uganda has made new discoveries in the Victoria Nile Delta off the north-eastern shore of Lake Albert while Ghana and Equatorial Guinea, among other African nations, have announced sizeable new finds.
- In East Asia additional oil reserves are proving somewhat harder to find. However, demand growth outstrips that of anywhere else internationally, forcing the region to become ever more reliant on imported supplies. China has announced some new finds offshore from Qinhuangdao in the Bohai Gulf and there have been some new finds in the Timor Sea, leading to some arguments over control of these finds between East Timor (Timor Leste) and Indonesia. Smaller finds have also occurred offshore Malaysia and Indonesia.

The oil being discovered now is often difficult to get at – either geologically (including the fact that offshore exploration and drilling is expensive despite improved technology while other deposits involve drilling through rock) or politically as many of the new finds are in countries with problematic domestic political situations, suffering internal conflict or simply lacking an adequate infrastructure to export the oil after extraction. Despite this, new finds are being exploited worldwide in ever more places. What this all means is that in terms of transportation of oil more tankers will be calling at more ports; as the SLOCs become ever more crowded and develop an ever greater number of branch lines to new sources of supply, the potential threats to the smooth and uninterrupted movement of oil are increasing. The potential number of global choke points continues to grow and oil wealth is spreading to unstable countries, leading to a resurgence of conflict and piracy.

The other new source of oil is from countries whose oil was not previously available on the international market. Russia is the prime example. Following the collapse of the Soviet Union, the Russian Federation has become a petro superpower, pumping more oil than Saudi Arabia. In 2008 Saudi Arabia produced 9.26 mn bpd while Russia produced 9.36 mn. However, Saudi Arabia is technically the bigger exporter, with oil shipments accounting for over 90 per cent of the kingdom's total oil, while Russia, with a sizeable domestic industrial base (and by some measures the world's third largest energy user), exports only 70 per cent of its production and refines the remaining 30 per cent locally for domestic use. Still, oil has changed Russia fundamentally as oil-related wealth has swept across the country transforming the post-Communist economy into a Russian version of a petro state. Importantly, the entry of Russian oil onto the global market has occurred in parallel with the rise of the economies of China and East Asia. Since the turn of the century Russia has accounted for 80 per cent of the growth in oil production outside OPEC. The increase in Russia's output in the early part of the decade matched the growth in demand from China and India almost barrel for barrel.

Russia is still expanding production with vast amounts of money being directed into large oil, and gas, projects. Importantly, given that the major growth in demand for oil is coming from East Asia, many of these new projects are in Siberia and Russia's Far Eastern territories between Siberia and the Pacific Ocean, including Sakhalin Island. Sakhalin, with especially close access to Japan but also to the Korean peninsula and north-east China, is now a classic 'resource economy' (since two large consortiums signed contracts to explore for oil and gas off the north-east coast of the island in 1996) relying on oil and gas exports. With a population of only approximately 600,000 people, Sakhalin has undergone an oil boom that now accounts for over 80 per cent of the island's economy and involves major Russian and international oil companies such as ExxonMobil and Shell tapping into the island's estimated 14 bn barrels of oil (and 96 trn cubic feet of gas).

At the same time as the emergence of a host of new oil exporters across the globe to complement and compete with the Middle East as well as the emergence of Russia (and to a lesser extent the former Soviet republics of Central Asia) as a petro state, the world has seen the most continued increased demand for oil from East Asia. The landscape and the geography of the international oil business has changed with new petro superpowers (including Russia, the Central Asian republics and other states such as Venezuela and Angola as well as the Middle East) and new petro superconsumers (such as China and India). That many of the new petro states[4] rely on an uninterrupted flow of oil-derived revenues for their economic and political stability while the consuming states, such as China, rely on uninterrupted flows of oil into their economies, both to maintain stability and growth, the uninterrupted delivery of oil will be a major continuing concern into the twenty-first century.

The Crucial Role of East Asia

The uninterrupted movement and supply of oil has clearly become an issue of globalisation. Without uninterrupted oil supplies China cannot function as the cheap labour workshop of the world; the West cannot consume at the rate it currently does; and the oil producer economies – from the Middle East to Russia and Central Asia to Latin America and Africa – cannot develop as they hope to. Oil has been crucial to the globalist consensus of the consumption economy – the East produces, the West consumes; the East becomes wealthier from this trade and so then begins to raise living standards and consume more itself. Production and consumption are linked by an endless line of tankers sailing between the two, literally oiling the wheels of globalisation.

As the global economy has shifted on its axis from West to East, East Asia, and China in particular, are concerned about any interruption to their oil supplies. That North America and Western Europe are worried about oil supplies is an older story. Everywhere in the world is now increasingly dependent on and linked to the continued rise of East Asia as a producer, investor, consumer and (for some) role model. China (as well as Japan, South Korea, Taiwan and most of South East Asia) are all countries with limited amounts of natural energy resources yet they are all large-scale manufacturers and require vast inputs of energy and raw materials to maintain their growth.

Table 1.2 **Top fifteen countries with largest oil consumption, 2008**

Country	Consumption ('000 barrels daily)	Share of total global consumption (%)
USA	19,419	22.5
China	7,999	9.6
Japan	4,845	5.6
India	2,882	3.4
Russian Federation	2,797	3.3
Germany	2,505	3.0
Brazil	2,397	2.8
Canada	2,295	2.7
South Korea	2,291	2.7
Saudi Arabia	2,224	2.6
Mexico	2,039	2.3
France	1,930	2.3
Iran	1,730	2.1
UK	1,704	2.1
Italy	1,691	2.0

Source: *BP Statistical Review of World Energy*, June 2009

China, a one-party dictatorship, has come to fear, indeed almost obsess, about its continued uninterrupted oil supplies – the country currently maintains a strategic reserve of approximately 102 mn barrels which the Beijing government intends to increase by a further 170 mn barrels. The government only initiated the plan to more than double their reserves in 2004 when they deemed the issue to be becoming crucial to maintaining a momentum of economic growth. A combined total of 272 mn barrels would raise the country's strategic reserve inventory from its current extremely low period of a fortnight to closer to forty days if consumption remains at around 2008 levels (i.e. 7.8 mn bpd) – still well short of the IEA-suggested ninety days of reserves.

With little domestic oil available, the ruling Chinese Communist Party (CCP) knows that any significant and/or long-term interruption to oil supplies would leave the country hostage to foreign interests while a prolonged interruption would cause chaos in its manufacturing industry and throw millions, if not hundreds of millions, out of work, on to the streets and perhaps into social protest. The economics are obvious – China's net oil imports were approximately 3.9 mn bpd in 2008, making it the third largest net oil importer in the world behind the USA and Japan. China is now importing approximately half its oil needs, and domestic production is not growing fast enough to compensate and restrain this growing percentage dependence on imports. Additionally, many of China's oil fields are showing severe signs of ageing and underinvestment. PetroChina's largest (and flagship) Daqing oil field in northern Heilongjiang province, which has been in production since 1963, began cutting its crude oil output by an annual 7 per cent for seven years from 2004 to try to extend its productive life.

South Korea and Taiwan have similar worries – for Seoul there is the need to maintain its manufacturing industry and heavy military expenditure given the perceived threat from across the Demilitarized Zone (DMZ) to the North. South Korea remains the fourth largest economy in Asia and the thirteenth largest in the world, and its politicians aim to improve that ranking: successful 2007 presidential candidate Lee Myung-bak's popular '747 Plan' for the nation included a 7 per cent annual growth in GDP aimed at making Korea the world's seventh largest economy.[5] However, Korea relies heavily on exports and is among the world's top exporters. Korea's conglomerates, or *chaebols*, such as Samsung, Hyundai, LG and SK Group, are now internationally known. The country remains a major manufacturer of cars, ships (the world's largest), electronics and IT. But this reliance on exports combined with a resources-light country means that the economy is almost totally reliant on imported oil and the health of the global economy – in early February 2009 the Korean Won had fallen 31 per cent in value against the US dollar in the preceding year. The Korean economy shrank 3.4 per cent year-on-year in the fourth quarter of 2008, while the benchmark stock index lost almost 41 per cent of its value. Seoul must deal with the constant threat from Pyongyang to the North, which, among other problems, ensures that no land-based pipeline flows into the South, making the country entirely dependent on seaborne oil supplies.

Box 1.1   World Without Oil: Possible Scenarios for East Asia

China

- Rapid slowdown in manufacturing = widespread unemployment.
- Unemployment + rising petrol pump prices + rising utility bills/blackouts in major cities = social discontent and disenchantment with the ruling CCP.
- Social discontent could lead to a severe crackdown by alarmed ruling elite.
- Slowdown in manufacturing + social discontent and government response = flight of capital and collapse of China–Hong Kong stock markets.
- Oil shortages could lead China or Japan more aggressively to force the already highly contentious sovereignty issues around the Senkaku/Diaoyutai Islands in the East China Sea and their potential oil and gas reserves.
- Interruptions of supply from Central Asia could heighten tensions on China's western borders and also reignite discontent in Xinjiang province.

Japan

- Any prolonged interruption to oil supplies would eventually deplete Japan's reserves, leading to shortages and economic contraction.
- Tokyo's traditionally delicate balance between geopolitics and its energy needs would be viewed by many as untenable in the future.
- There is the possibility of renewed military manoeuvres by Japan to secure oil-supply routes and a tougher negotiating stance on pipelines.
- Any real or supposed rearmament or heightened military activity by Japan could spark conflict with China and a regional arms race.
- Domestically extremist parties in Japan could move to break the post-World War II liberal consensus.

South Korea
- Slowdown in manufacturing = unemployment.
- Rising fuel bills and unemployment lead to protests against government.
- Shortage of energy = no ability to export energy to economically ailing North Korea, leading to the collapse of the DPRK regime and a subsequent political and refugee crisis, as well as financial demand from the North on the South.
- Perceived weakness and demonstrations in South Korea may lead to exacerbated tensions across the DMZ. Possibility of heightened tensions between South and North Korea if Pyongyang were to seek to take advantage of the situation = significant expansion in military spending and an arms race on the Korean peninsula.
- Any increase in tension between the two Koreas could mean American involvement on Seoul's behalf (there are approximately 28,500 US military personnel stationed in South Korea) and heightened tensions with Japan (where a further 47,000 US troops are based).

Taiwan
- Shortage of oil threatens economic growth = unemployment and deteriorating standard of living for many.
- There is the likelihood of political turmoil and a rise in support for advocates of Taiwanese independence and/or advocates of greater unity with mainland China.
- Seeking to divert attention from domestic trouble, Beijing may act increasingly belligerently towards Taiwan, potentially sparking cross-Straits tensions and conflict that draws the US and others into a cross-Straits conflict.

Taiwan is an island with some coal deposits but only insignificant petroleum and natural gas deposits. It too is reliant on seaborne deliveries of oil as it is cut off from pipeline routes. At the same time it has an extremely uneasy relationship with the Beijing government and mainland China that adds to its oil woes as it must maintain a large military.

Finally there is Japan, which has been a developed and industrialised economy for longer than its East Asian neighbours and so, to an extent, has learned to live with oil import dependency. Japan relies on the Middle East for approximately 88 per cent of its oil supplies. Japan has also been a rich country for longer than its emerging neighbours and so has been able to build up longer-term relations with suppliers, advanced infrastructure across its islands and a full 90 days' reserve. Japan's longer-term wealth has also allowed it to establish and grow its national fleet of oil tankers and merchant marine. Japan's earlier industrialisation meant that it was in a position to take stock of its oil dependency in the wake of the oil crises of the 1970s, when it began seriously to plan alternatives. Japan's Ministry of Economy, Trade and Industry (METI) has long been developing long-term energy plans with the aim of reducing the country's reliance on imported oil and increasing the share of natural gas and nuclear power in Japan's primary energy mix. These efforts have been partially successful, with gas consumption increasing and oil slightly decreasing, but it should be noted that, while still wealthy and the second largest economy in the world, Japan has been in repeated recessions since the bursting of the so-called Japanese 'bubble economy' in 1990, which has slowed growth.

The supply of oil must be preserved in East Asia – Beijing pledges to maintain social harmony and the Communist Party pledges to remain in power. Taiwan and South Korea are relatively newly formed democracies and their ruling administrations are extremely fragile when faced with economic downturns. The interruption of oil supplies by sea to East Asia could see turmoil break out in China and exacerbate tension across both the DMZ between the two Koreas and the Taiwan Straits between the two Chinas.

Oil supply is also a source of wider potential global conflict. Developed countries that cannot access oil may increasingly feel themselves justified in enforcing supplies. Developing countries whose continued growth is in part predicated on the uninterrupted supply of oil to their emerging economies could continue to move to protect their supplies. Already many in the West are concerned about China's involvement in Africa as well as closer to home in Central Asia, Burma and Pakistan. These new diplomatic, investment, aid and military connections are realigning the way the world thinks and they are largely driven by the intense competition for resources.

However, oil has also become a global unifier at a certain level. The unparalleled coalition of navies involved in the joint anti-piracy patrols around the Horn of Africa is an interesting phenomenon. It arises from a common enemy and one that refuses to fit the usual profile of worrisome states, rogue regimes and/or ideological movements such as Al-Qaeda – the pirates have no friends and seemingly no cause or allegiances beyond obtaining ransom payments. Prior to the rise of the piracy threat off the Somali coast no other protagonist could have brought the navies of the United States, the nations of the EU, NATO, China, India, Iran, Japan and Russia to work together towards a common cause – combating the interruption to the SLOCs around the Horn of Africa. The pirates are a common enemy who have the ability to inspire nations to work together as nothing else in recent times except perhaps disaster relief. In particular, the non-traditional role of nations such as China and India in multilateral patrols of the seas reveals the growing shift East of oil deliveries and a growing concern among the nations of East Asia to ensure those deliveries. This is part of a wider shift of gravity in the economics of oil.

CHAPTER TWO

The Shift East

Monday 6 October 2008 – The Singapore Straits

Except when loading and unloading, oil tankers like the Shinyo Ocean
rarely stop. Once loaded with their cargo of oil they invariably sail
non-stop directly to their port of delivery. If the sea is calm, a fully
loaded supertanker can cruise at approximately 15 knots, or around
17–18 miles per hour, meaning a tanker can sail approximately 400
miles a day fully loaded. The tankers are floating communities with a
population of, on average, twenty to twenty-five crew, who are often at
sea together for a month on a typical voyage from the oil fields of the
Middle East to the oil-thirsty industrial zones of East Asia. The vessel's
galley is stocked with provisions; they can make their own fresh water
and have a surprisingly wide range of home comforts from DVDs and
duty-free beer to table tennis and StairMasters to keep fit.

Rarely, if ever, were we totally alone at sea – invariably there was
at least one other ship on the horizon. Sailing west to east through
the Malacca Straits and into the South China Sea there is a constant
procession of vessels laden with oil, gas and other commodities, as
well as empty container ships heading to East Asia to collect the
manufactured goods the world's shops and consumers require. In the
east to west sea lanes the reverse is the case – container ships are loaded
down with the standardised oblong metal containers that move goods
from the factories of Asia to the shops of the West, while the empty
oil tankers, depleted bulk carriers riding higher out of the water and
liquefied natural gas (LNG) carriers, with their trademark spherical
tanks on deck to hold the gas, sail past on their way to refuel and
repeat their voyage East once again.

The Shinyo Ocean *keeps up a steady pace day and night, relentlessly moving across the charts, ever closer to our destination on Taiwan's western coast. It's a repetitive life at sea – breakfast at 7 a.m., lunch at noon and dinner at 7 p.m. For those of us aboard without assigned tasks there's nothing much to do but study the horizon and lie around reading. For the crew there are a multiplicity of tasks to undertake from maintaining the engines and monitoring the radar through to the thankless job of maintaining the ship through painting and repainting in the never-ending cycle of keeping the elements and salt at bay. Every few hours we check in with the bridge for a cup of tea with the captain and to examine the charts. Every time we've moved another half inch further west from Singapore and closer to Taiwan.*

A Shifting Centre of Gravity

At numerous conferences, and spread across newspaper headlines and magazine articles around the world, there is a general consensus that the world's centre of gravity is shifting eastwards – economically at least and, to a lesser extent perhaps, militarily, culturally and politically. In the case of oil and its transportation this is most certainly the case. The most important trend in global affairs and in the international oil industry is the shift in economic and political power towards East and South Asia. However, this shift is in large part predicated on the Asian nations' continued economic growth and rising wealth; for that to occur, they need oil and with only limited domestic reserves they need to import it. If you accept the World Bank's argument that both China and India, clearly the two most populous and fast-growing of the Asian economies, can sustain growth rates of between 8 and 10 per cent for another ten to fifteen years, and will then continue growing beyond that time period at slightly reduced rates, they will treble their economic output.[1] As the World Bank has described it, this shift is the 'next wave of globalisation'.

How much of this 'shift of gravity' or 'next wave of globalisation' is real economically is arguable. Despite the phenomenal growth rates in India and China their starting bases were relatively low, and while this has meant undoubted improvements in the living standards of hundreds of millions of people it has not fundamentally changed the world balance of economic power. According to the International Monetary Fund (IMF), Asia's share of global GDP has only increased slightly overall in the last twenty years while the United States and the EU have only slipped marginally, indicating that the relative balance of economic power remains approximately the same globally.[2] However, within Asia there has been a noticeable shift in the internal economic balance of power away from long-depressed Japan towards rapidly developing and industrialising China and India. Where the shifting balance is even more noticeable is in oil consumption – in this economic sphere Asia has indeed drastically altered the global balance of consumption.

As a general rule, those areas of the globe where consumption of commodities and raw materials is growing fastest are also the 'hot zones' of global production. Across a range of commodity sectors East Asia, and notably China, have become major consumers. This includes not just oil and gas but also other key commodities such as metals, iron ore, coal, phosphates as well as rubber and cotton. For China, and the wider East Asian region, to be the world's leading producers they need massive inputs of raw materials. The region is also rapidly urbanising as consumer wealth is rising and so needs additional sources of energy and commodities to feed its own construction booms and domestic demand for power, whether it be petrol for cars or electricity for air conditioners.

The simple fact is that this shift in global production accompanied by a rising domestic demand in China and across East Asia (and in India and South East Asia too) has led to a growing demand and to East Asia taking an increasing share of global oil exports. The United States may still be far and away the world's largest consumer of oil but China is catching up – fast. China became a net importer of oil in the mid-1990s and by 2002 was equal to Japan and lagging only behind the USA in consuming over 5 mn bpd and becoming the world's fifth biggest importer of oil at nearly 2 mn bpd. Just a year later China's consumption was 5.6 mn bpd as the manufacturing economy continued to surge – an unprecedented growth of 19 per cent year-on-year, easily outstripping previously recorded growth rates in either the USA or Japan.

Even with a maturing of the Chinese economy that may 'cool' somewhat going forward coupled with a slowdown in demand from the Western nations for consumer goods in the face of economic recession from late 2008, China's oil import dependency is here to stay and growing due to limited domestic reserves. The IEA has predicted that China's oil import dependency could rise to 75 per cent by 2030 from approximately 50 per cent now.[3] This outlook is supported by China's own economic planners. According to China's customs authorities, the nation imported 159 mn tonnes of crude oil in 2007 and produced 187 mn tonnes, with its oil-import dependence reaching 51 per cent for the first time. This has led the economic planners of Beijing to exceed even the IEA estimate and predict that China's crude oil imports will more than double, resulting in an oil dependency ratio of 80 per cent in 2030.[4] Quite simply it is impossible for China and the economies of East, South East and South Asia to continue to grow economically without further increasing their dependence on foreign oil. This means that with China's rapid industrialisation and growing domestic consumer demand the country's thirst for imported oil is expected to quadruple from less than 2 mn bpd in 2004 to nearly 8 mn bpd by 2020, of which approximately 60–70 per cent will have to be imported – a rate of growth unprecedented in history.

These growth statistics and projections indicate that securing constant and uninterrupted supplies of oil internationally into China will be a prime economic security issue for Beijing and simultaneously ensure that China will remain increasingly important on the global oil markets in terms of price, investment and transportation. Some analysts predict even greater growth rates. Dr Fatih Birol, chief economist at the IEA, recently told an audience at the Council on Foreign Relations that 'China will import about 10 million barrels per day of oil around 2015, and 13 million barrels per day in 2030, similar to the United States.' In essence, he noted, 'China, in terms of oil imports, will be the United States of tomorrow.'[5]

Prior to the rise of China and East Asia as major consumers of oil the shipment of oil by sea was primarily (but not exclusively) predicated on Middle Eastern production being sent to North America and Europe. As a consequence of this most tanker companies were US or EU owned (though not necessarily flagged – see chapter 7, 'Flags of Convenience').

Table 2.1 **Projected oil consumption growth for selected Asian countries, 2008–2018**

Country	Forecast oil consumption growth 2008–2018 (% bpd)
China	47.4
India	48.7
Indonesia	22.1
Japan	−11.6
Malaysia	16.5
Pakistan	27.1
Philippines	26.8
Singapore	31.9
South Korea	4.3
Taiwan	21.7
Thailand	24.9
Vietnam	76.5

Source: National economic forecasts, IEA, Business Monitor International

However, as the shift in demand has moved increasingly eastwards so has the ownership, control and manning of oil tankers. Indeed, East Asian (and Singaporean) shares of the total global controlled fleet exceed their shares of global trade. For instance, South Korea controls 3.6 per cent of the global fleet and accounts for 2.6 per cent of world trade; Hong Kong 3.2 per cent and 2.6 per cent respectively, and Singapore 2.8 per cent and 2 per cent. This ratio of fleet control being larger than trade share is naturally more difficult for larger and more highly productive countries that are not entrepôt economies such as Hong Kong and Singapore. For instance, America accounted for 11.4 per cent of world trade in 2008 but controlled only 3.8 per cent of the global fleet (i.e. as a percentage share of the world fleet owned in terms of dead weight tonnage). By contrast China accounted for 7.8 per cent of world trade and 8.2 per cent of the global fleet.

Table 2.2 **Ten largest independent oil tanker companies, 2009**

Tanker company	Headquartered	No. of tankers	dwt mn
Mitsui OSK	Japan	108	14.1
Frontline	Norway	59	11.4
Teekay	Canada	99	11.1
NITC	Iran	43	9.6
Overseas Shipholding Group	USA	90	8.3
NYK Line	Japan	28	8.2
Tanker Pacific Management	Singapore	56	7.0
AET	Malaysia	57	6.9
Euronav	Belgium	28	6.6
DS Schiffahrt	Germany	30	5.8
Total		**598**	**89.0**
Total independent fleet		4391	352.2

Table 2.3 **Ten largest oil company/state-owned oil tanker companies, 2009**

Tanker company	Headquartered	No. of tankers	dwt mn
Saudi Aramco	Saudi Arabia	28	7.4
China Shipping Group	China	78	4.9
National Shipping SA	Saudi Arabia	29	4.6
Sovcomflot	Russia	48	4.3
COSCO	China	33	4.2
Indian Government	India	44	4.1
Novoship	Russia	50	4.0
BP	UK	35	3.9
Kuwait Petroleum Group	Kuwait	20	3.2
China Changjiang Shipping	China	27	2.3
Total		**392**	**42.9**
Total oil co./state fleet		796	72.8

Source for both tables: *Intertanko*
Note: dwt = dead weight tonnage

Before all of this shift in oil demand, East Asia had for a long time been the acknowledged leader in world shipbuilding, a pattern largely dictated by demographics and relatively low cost labour as well as government subsidy. Recently there has been a swift handover of the shipbuilding baton to China.

First, however, came Japan. From 1951 to 1972, 31.5 per cent of all loans made by the Japan Development Bank went on marine transportation.[6] Shipbuilding became a pillar industry for Japan after World War II, and one in which they would lead the world until the start of the twenty-first century. Demographics are key to shipyard fortunes. Japan had usurped Europe's position as the leading shipbuilding destination but Japan was soon to face competition from far nearer to home. By the time Japan lost its place at the top of the shipyard stakes the average age of those in the industry had passed forty, and rival nations had labour costs twenty times less than the world's second largest economy. Nowadays, the average Japanese shipbuilder is more than fifty years old.

Building Tankers: from the Clyde to Korea

Across the Sea of Japan, Chung Ju-Yung was born in 1915 to an impoverished family. He was the eldest of eight, born in Asan, in what would become the Democratic People's Republic of Korea (DPRK). After a tough upbringing Chung fled the rural poverty of the north for the burgeoning commercial city of Seoul aged just sixteen. He financed his 120-mile trek by selling one of his father's cows. That life-long guilt would prompt him to send 1,500 cattle to North Korea as a humanitarian gesture in 1998. By 1937 he had saved enough cash to set up a rice shop. However, Korea's colonial masters, the Japanese, shut this business down. Undeterred, he became a truck driver, running a delivery service before establishing a car repair garage. After the end of World War II and Korea's liberation from the Japanese, aged thirty-one, he founded the Hyundai empire, which would encompass construction, engineering and cars by the end of the 1960s.

Then in 1972 Chung took a gamble. He booked an order for a supertanker for C.T. Tung, the father of Hong Kong's first post-colonial chief executive, C.H. Tung, before he had even built his own shipyard.

Despite this he delivered the vessel on time. The shipbuilding division of Hyundai Heavy Industries was born and South Korea was on track to become a world-beating shipbuilder. *Chaebols* such as Samsung and Daewoo rapidly became internationally recognised shipbuilding brands. Today, Hyundai Heavy Industries is the world's largest shipbuilder with ten huge dry docks and three other shipbuilding subsidiaries. Korea surpassed Japan at the top of the shipyards league table in 2000, yet no sooner had it hit the peak than it was looking over its shoulders at the next challenger, whose rise was once again caused by demographics.

'I look forward to the day when our country is no longer the largest shipbuilding nation in the world.'[7] On the face of it, an odd thing for a vice-president of the world's largest shipbuilder, Hyundai Heavy Industries, to be saying at the height of its supremacy some five years ago. But think of it another way: shipbuilding is essentially factory work on a very large scale – metal is cut and assembled into a giant framework. Over the past century, the sight of massive ships sliding down slipways has engendered national pride across the world from Glasgow to Philadelphia, but countries mature, and eventually become post-industrial. Shipbuilding is, in many ways, a meter to understanding how a country is progressing economically. It takes a manufacturing powerhouse to become a serious shipbuilder in the first place and likewise it takes a mature economy with higher wages and different skill sets to dispense with this industry. It is usually one of the very last heavy industries to be closed.

At the start of the twentieth century Britain ruled the waves but Germany was fast catching up, and by the 1920s was on a par with the UK. Indeed, it has been argued that the dramatic rise of hard-working German shipyard workers in ports like Hamburg and Bremen was an indirect cause of World War I. After World War I Europe continued to hold sway on the shipbuilding front. Then came Japan; latterly South Korea.

Yet, like Japan before it, South Korea is growing up – shipbuilding is no longer considered an attractive career option for Korea's hip and educated youth, and the average age of workers has crossed the forty mark while their costs are increasingly uncompetitive to many emerging nations, especially China. Korean shipbuilding wages are now seven times those of their Chinese counterparts; the inevitable handover of shipbuilding prowess is happening now. Korea's time at the top was very brief.

Box 2.1 The Birth of the Supertanker: A Brief History

Rather quaintly, the oil industry still thinks in barrels but oil is now transported in vast tankers in gigantic holds. In the nineteenth century oil was moved by sea on break-bulk boats and barges laden with forty-US-gallon wooden barrels but these leaked, weighed 64 pounds (fully 20 per cent of the total weight of a full barrel) and could only be used one way. Barrels were expensive too. When Russia's oil industry first started to ship oil, barrels accounted for half the cost of petroleum production.[8] In the later nineteenth century American, British and Belgian shipbuilders experimented with sail-driven tankers and then steamers but no designs were found to be either efficient, in terms of the amount of oil they could carry, or safe. It was Ludvig and Robert Nobel, brothers of Alfred Nobel and the founders of the powerful Branobel oil company in the boom town of Baku, who conquered the problems of fumes, fire, ventilation and the tendency of oil to expand and contract as the temperature changes. The Nobels' twin-hulled *Zoroaster* was built in Gothenburg, making its first run in 1878 from Baku to Astrakhan on the Volga River. The *Zoroaster* was a success but the Nobels refused to patent its design and so it was widely studied and copied. Branobel steadily built up a fleet of tankers in Baku. They refined the design further and then commissioned single-hull tankers. It was not a totally smooth process – in 1881, the *Zoroaster*'s sister-ship, the *Nordenskjöld*, exploded in Baku while taking on kerosene. By the early years of the twentieth century the Nobel brothers were building tankers that were powered by internal combustion engines rather than steam – vessels that could carry 750 long tons of refined oil.

Oil had started moving east on water early in the 1880s. The oil importer Marcus Samuel and a ship owner and broker by the name of Fred Lane decided they wanted to move Russian oil to Asia via the Suez Canal. However, the Suez Canal Company had banned ships carrying oil, claiming it was too risky. Samuel commissioned three ships specifically designed to transport oil through the canal safely. The Canal Company agreed they could transit and the first tankers of the Tank Syndicate, the forerunner of today's Royal Dutch Shell, sailed with oil for newly built depots in Bangkok, Batavia, Hong

Kong, Kobe, Saigon, Singapore and Shanghai. For the first time a
European oil company could compete with America's Standard Oil
in the Asian market. Standard Oil crossed the Pacific and had up
until then enjoyed a monopoly on the East Asian oil trade.

Fig. 2.1 The *Jahre Viking,* formerly the *Seawise Giant* – the longest ship
ever built, as well as the greatest deadweight tonnage ever recorded

Tankers played a crucial role in World War II, keeping both sides of
the conflict supplied. After the war, tanker sizes started to increase
significantly until some vessels became too large for the Suez Canal
and started to use the Cape of Good Hope to travel from west
to east. Oil companies and their customers realised that there was
a simple economic law at work – the larger the tanker, the more
affordable it was to move crude oil long distances. In 1958, the US
shipping magnate Daniel K. Ludwig built a tanker that broke the
100,000 long tons of heavy displacement record and in 1979 Japan's
Sumitomo Heavy Industries built the world's largest ever tanker,
the *Seawise Giant,* which weighed into the record books at 564,763
dwt with a length of 1,504 feet. The *Seawise Giant* was too large – it
could not call at most ports, never carried a full load and was too
big to traverse some of the world's key shipping arteries, including

the English Channel. Despite the mixed history of the *Seawise Giant*, the era of the supertanker and the great oil shipping magnates, such as Aristotle Onassis of Greece and Sir Y.K. Pao of Hong Kong, had arrived.

Now there are more than 5,500 oil tankers of all shapes and sizes sailing the seas.

Sino Shipbuilding Supremacy

Aware of its growing dependence on oil imports to further economic growth China has embarked on a dual build-up of its shipyards and by extension its merchant fleet to allow it greater control over its supplies. The goals are twinned – to be the world's largest shipbuilder by 2015 as well as carrying 50 per cent of all the country's oil imports on Chinese vessels by that date. The scale of the yards under construction in China dwarfs even the mammoth ten-dock-strong Hyundai Heavy Industries in South Korea. China's rush to the top has been miraculous in terms of ascending the technology ladder. Huge amounts of money have been spent on dock construction and research and development. There have been court cases in South Korea relating to technology transfer theft, with workers there accused of passing on design secrets to the Chinese. 'There's nothing so powerful in China as a Xerox machine,' confided one British naval engineer.

China had been a second-tier shipbuilder until the beginning of the twenty-first century, churning out around one million compensated gross tonnes (CGT) of ships a year from 1997 to 2000. Then, in 2004, business seriously started to pick up as Beijing made a series of official pronouncements detailing its aims to boost tanker ownership to 50 per cent of crude imports (up from 15 per cent) and to be the world's leading shipbuilder. The timing of this announcement back in 2004 was remarkably fortuitous as it coincided with one of shipping's greatest boom periods.

Shipping is one of the ultimate boom and bust cyclical industries. In October 2003 the conditions were ripe for one of the most protracted upswings in the history of shipping – what the London shipbroker Clarkson would describe as the greatest shipping boom since records began in 1774. Extraordinary demand by China for raw materials, in particular iron ore, combined with limited port infrastructure in mining countries such as Australia and Brazil, started the climb of shipping rates.[9] North America and Europe's insatiable demand for cheap Chinese manufactured products saw demand for container shipping East to West also scale the heights while oil demand the world over rose sharply. In short, there were too few ships to accommodate the huge pent-up demand, led by China's oil and commodity import requirements and the country's ability to produce cheap exports for overseas markets.

The shipping press invariably uses the term 'lemmings' to describe the ability of ship owners to further their own demise by piling *en masse* into shipyards to order ships at high prices that ultimately swung the supply/demand equation against them. This particular cycle was different in the stratospheric earnings the industry garnered and the length of time it lasted. Earnings per ship in US dollars regularly soared into six-digits-a-day territory over a five-year period, far longer than the traditional previous one-year upturns. This gave ship owners the misplaced confidence to order vessels at record prices and in record volumes. Shipbuilders, citing high material costs, especially for steel plate, raised their prices to the point where the price of new-build VLCCs were at twice their historic averages, coming in at highs of US\$130 mn and upwards per ship.

Existing shipyards throughout the world expanded their facilities during these glorious times, while new shipbuilding entities entered the fray, especially in China, where at the height of the excess there were around 200 'greenfield' yards. Companies with no history of shipbuilding rushed to list on stock exchanges across the region even before they had built their own dry dock, let alone their first ship.

By 2006 China had surpassed Japan in terms of ship orders received and accepted. Powerful Hong Kong owners shunned old business partners in South Korea and Japan in favour of making patriotic orders in China. Greece, the largest ship-owning nation, saw the bargains on offer and came to China too, while Chinese state-owned enterprises placed massive billion-dollar deals with emerging Chinese shipyards.

Fig. 2.2 Dalian Shipyard – China's shipbuilding industry is in the midst
of a massive expansion

News constantly trickled through of more huge new facilities being
built up and down the Chinese coastline. The number of privately
held shipyards exceeded their state-run counterparts. By 2008 China
had surpassed Japan in ships delivered for the year, accounting for
29.5 per cent of all ships built in 2008, according to the Ministry of
Communications in Beijing.[10] The Chinese had also mastered the gamut
of technologically challenging ships. The delivery of a liquefied natural
gas (LNG) carrier by Shanghai's Hudong-Zhonghua Shipbuilding
in 2008 completed the climb up the technology ladder for China's
shipyards (with the exception of luxury cruise ships which are still the
preserve of Europe's dwindling shipbuilders). Gas ships represent the
toughest cargo ship design and construction challenges and although
the delivery of the LNG carrier was late (and it has since experienced
numerous problems) it was still a significant landmark in China's ascent
to the top of the international shipbuilding table.

Since 2008 the shipping market has nosedived dramatically, entering
its darkest phase for a generation in line with the global economic
downturn. A concomitant downturn in cargo demand was made doubly

dangerous by bankers' sudden inability to splash credit to the industry. Orders were cancelled and many shipyards went bust. Shipping's irrational exuberance was found out and ended badly for many.

However, Beijing placed shipbuilding as a central tenet of its 2009 US$586 bn stimulus package. Loans were provided, consolidation encouraged and state-run shipping lines coerced to place more orders at home to keep the domestic yards up and running. The downturn in shipping could well hasten, not deter, China's rise to the top, thanks to central government support and encouragement. A decade ago there was just one shipyard in China capable of building VLCCs, technically demanding giant vessels whose design requires much stress testing. Each longer than the Eiffel Tower is high, these are the primary means of shifting large loads of oil. Now, the country has a double-digit number of yards easily capable of building these mammoth ship types.

The difference, going forward, between South Korea and China, in terms of how long the latter can remain at the top of the shipbuilding pile, once again comes down to demographics. China still has a greater supply of cheap labour coming from poorer inland provinces. So while other nations – led by Vietnam and India – will come to play a more important role in global shipbuilding in the coming years, no one will be in a position to challenge China for at least a generation.

China's Tanker Fleet

Mainland China, excluding Hong Kong, now owns thirty-seven VLCCs, a figure that is set to hit sixty-three by the end of 2010. With maritime oil supply chain security being prioritised and fast-tracked by Beijing, this target total may well be met ahead of schedule.

China's fleet carried only 6.7 per cent of the country's crude oil imports in 2000, but that share surged to 20 per cent in 2005. The 50 per cent goal, as outlined back in 2004, is likely to be hit four years ahead of schedule in 2011. Apart from East Asian neighbours such as South Korea and Japan, very few other nations can boast such a strong national tanker portfolio. India, for instance, is playing a belated game of catch up, wary that currently only 15 per cent of all oil India imports by ship arrives on Indian-owned vessels. Given this situation, what worries independent tanker owners greatly is how the big Chinese tanker operators could go about sealing off the market to real international competition, contrary to World Trade Organization (WTO) rules.

Mao Shijia, the Managing Director at the state-owned tanker company China Shipping Development, has called for a Chinese VLCC 'pool' to share risks and achieve better scales of economy. Mr Mao would also like to see tanker owners go beyond their traditional seaborne remit and further their oil supply chain footprint, extending interests into terminals, pipelines and rail. Speaking at a spring 2009 conference in Shanghai, Mao said that the coming together of China's big three state-owned oil conglomerates and big three state-owned shipping firms was a good and inevitable development:[11] 'I think there is a possibility for upstream and downstream businesses to collaborate together to consolidate business.'[12] This talk of Chinese partnership worried some ship owners in the room, who voiced concerns over possible protectionism being exercised by China's shipping majors. Furthermore, receiving facilities for all these new ships have been massively built up this decade as part of China's wider infrastructure expansion.

Oil Terminals

Port development as a whole has seen wide-ranging changes along China's once rugged coastline. Now concrete, bollards and container cranes vie with pipelines and conveyor belts on China's increasingly congested seaboard.

It is not just oil demand that is changing China's ports. One in two containers, the big metal boxes that moves the bulk of the world's goods around the seas, handled internationally spend time in China at some point on their journey.[13] China's ports handled 126 mn containers in 2008, up from just 25 mn in 2000. Likewise, China contributed approximately 78 per cent to the total increase in the world's iron ore and steel output in the first decade of the twenty-first century. It imported around 70 mn tonnes of iron ore back in 2000, a figure that hit 440 mn tonnes in 2008 and could surpass 600 mn tonnes in 2010.

Both these facts have seen big-port infrastructure being built up to accommodate imports and exports by sea. Oil demand has been at the vanguard of this development. China's port authorities have been reformed and decentralised and have had huge sums lavished on new facilities.

Before the 1990s China only needed domestic oil shipping and its terminals were very small, usually of 30,000–50,000 dwt handling capacity. With rapidly growing demand, China became a net oil importer and by 2000 was importing more than 60 mn tonnes of crude oil, mostly from the Middle East in much larger oil carrying vessels. But at that time, there were only three large oil terminals of 150,000–200,000 dwt capacity in the entire country. They were located at Ningbo in eastern China, in neighbouring Zhoushan and in Maoming in southern China's Guangdong province. Since 2000 China has dramatically sped up the construction of large oil terminals with a capacity above 200,000 dwt. By the end of 2007 China had built ten oil terminals of 200,000 dwt capacity and above, with 17 mn tonnes of loading capacity and 160.8 mn tonnes of unloading capacity.

The process continues. In the first half of 2009 the 300,000 dwt oil terminal in Qinglanshan in Eastern China's Fujian Province on the Taiwan Strait and the 300,000 dwt oil terminal in Yingkou, Liaoning Province in north-eastern China were put into operation. By the end of 2009 China had the capacity to handle 281.9 mn tonnes of oil.

In terms of the layout of these oil terminals, there are three clusters geographically: around the rim of the Bohai Gulf in north-eastern China, the Yangtze River Delta (YRD) in eastern China and the Pearl River Delta (PRD) in southern China near the border with Hong Kong. On the rim of the Bohai Gulf the ports of Dalian, Tianjin and Qingdao are the three leading players while Qinhuangdao, Jinzhou and Qingkou act as supporting ports. In the YRD the ports of Ningbo and Zhoushan play the main role while Shanghai and Nanjing act in supporting roles. In the PRD Quanzhou, Huizhou, Maoming, Zhanjiang and Yangpu ports each play an active role.

In the space of a decade China has built up an impressive infrastructure to handle its seaborne oil trade. No one has ever assembled a tanker fleet or string of terminals of such scale and quality in a similar time frame. Being in charge of its oil supply chain has been a national security priority in China since the mid-1990s. China has put money, labour and brainpower into making sure it can handle its own oil future. What it now has to take into consideration is the dangerous routes its ships have to take to get to the PRC – dangerous both geographically and, with the rise of piracy, societally. While China has fixed its domestic oil consumption aims, it must focus on overseas acquisition and here it is faced with competition from a host of other oil-hungry nations.

Table 2.4 **Major oil terminals in operation in China, 2009**

Name	Tonnage	Annual capacity (mt)	Production date	Remarks
Dagushan in Dalian	300,000	22.8	September 2004	510 m long, 25 m water depth, 12,000 t/hour
Huangdao in Qingdao	200,000	17	1990	498 m long, 21.3 m water depth
Daishan in Zhoushan	250,000	25	February 1996	Warehouse with 1.58 m tons of capacity
Cezidao in Zhoushan	300,000	20	February 2006	510 m long, with RMB730 mn investment
Suanshan* in Ningbo	250,000	20	1994	522 m long, 22.5 m water depth
Daxie Shihua in Ningbo	250,000	19	February 2006	485 m long, 25 m water depth, warehouse with 830,000 tons of capacity

Name	Tonnage	Annual capacity (mt)	Production date	Remarks
Mabianzhou in Huizhou	300,000	12	March 2007	490 m long, warehouse with 800,000 tonnes of capacity
Maoming in Guangdong	250,000	12	1994	Single-point anchoring unloading
Zhanjiang Port*	300,000	15	November 2002	470 m long, 18.6 m water depth
Yangpu Port	300,000	15	2007	Unloading 9,000 tonnes per hour
Caofeidian in Tangshan	300,000	20	August 2008	
Tianjin Port	300,000	20	October 2008	468 m long, 25 m water depth, RMB1.379 bn investment
Qingdao Port	300,000 –450,000	18	January 2008	520 m, 24 m water depth, RMB500 mn investment

Source: *Flynn Consulting* (Hong Kong)
Note: * Zhanjiang Port and Suanshan in Ningbo were originally designed to accommodate 150,000 dwt ships and later renovated to accommodate larger ships.

CHAPTER THREE

The Great Voyage

Tuesday 15 July 2008 – Fujairah Port, United Arab Emirates

It's searing hot outside. Thirty-eight degrees, says the ship's master, with humidity levels standing at a dizzying 97 per cent. The horizon, a mixture of sand and industrial complexes, shimmers in the heat. A brief sojourn outside, armed with binoculars to look at the queue of vessels, instantly makes clothing damp.

Back on the bridge, the air con purrs softly. The VLCC, one of the largest ships afloat at 300,000 dwt, is serenely calm. The sea is flat and we're in a holding pattern.

We are not alone. Here at Fujairah port, on the eastern seaboard of the United Arab Emirates, some 70 nautical miles from the Straits of Hormuz, there is a gaggle of vessels waiting to suck up the oil products piped into the assorted terminals for onward shipment across the globe.

We are at the deep anchorage 'Bravo' and have been here since dawn. To our left there are four ships lined up, to the right another three, and ahead of us, stretched beyond our enormous pipe-laden deck, are five more ships. All up, this assorted fleet costs in the region of US$1.2 bn. We're now number six in the queue. Each minute spent hanging around does not come cheap. At the time of boarding, in these heady pre-Lehman days of July 2008, oil prices are still over US$120 a barrel and tankers are similarly enjoying the fag end of the era of irrational exuberance. Our ship, for instance, is heading to Taiwan at a price of US$110,000 a day for the nineteen-day trip. This delay could be pricey.

'Look around you,' the ship's Indian captain, Arvind Halder, says, gesturing with his hand at our tanker encirclement. 'Who said oil has

47

peaked? Every time I come here there's more ships waiting to get in and suck up the oil products here.'

This growth in business has not gone unnoticed by local authorities who are halfway through an unsightly expansion of the port, large dredging spewing up into the ugly shoreline ahead.

'All Middle East terminals are like this,' Halder continues, rattling off a list of Arabic and Persian-sounding ports, his hand flitting from north to south on the chart below him. 'You guys in the West and increasingly the Asians just can't get enough of this stuff. That's why we have to kick our heels out here in this millpond so regularly.'

The VHF crackles to life. We're now fifth in the queue. There's a sense of impatience spreading across the crew, many of whom are destined to have their first shore leave in two months once the ship finally comes alongside.

'Come on,' the captain says, glancing at his watch. 'We've got time for a quick early lunch.' We hurry down to the galley where the friendly chef, who hails from Goa, has prepared another sumptuous, waist-expanding curry meal.

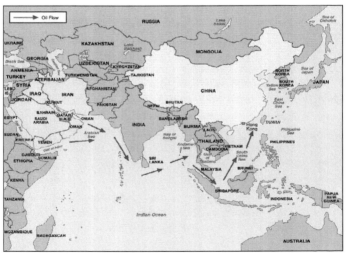

Fig. 3.1 Heading east – the critical sea lanes of communication

'People will have you believe that the world is moving beyond petroleum,' Halder says, scooping some dhal onto a still warm and soft roti bread. 'When you come to this slice of water and see the volume of ships and massive port complexes under construction you see for yourself we're all as addicted as we ever were to this commodity.'

The first officer, shirt neatly pressed, hair gelled and swept back, sidles up to the captain and tells him we're ready to go. The moustachioed captain swigs down some water, wipes his face, and heads back up to the bridge.

Two hours later we are moored alongside, vast mazes of pipes are primed and ready to insert 180,000 barrels of oil into our supertanker, a cargo worth more than US$20 million. Eight delighted crew head off for much-deserved and needed shore leave. Behind us in the haze the queue of ships stretches as far as the eye can see.

The Necessity of Oil Supply

Oil, and its procurement, it seems, is present in everything and everywhere. It is a determining factor in the relationships between more super-producer and super-consumer states than at any time previously. The competition for supplies becomes ever more intense.

No government in the world wants to be reliant on imported oil – it makes it potentially vulnerable economically, militarily, in terms of social stability and in terms of ultimate regime survival regardless of whether it is a democracy or a dictatorship. At the same time every government would dearly love to find and exploit additional reserves of oil on its national territory or in its national waters – 'resources windfalls'. Nevertheless, everyone accepts that, particularly for developing countries, there can often be a 'resources curse', the paradox of plenty. (Or, as the veteran Venezuelan diplomat, politician and lawyer Juan Pablo Pérez Alfonso put it, oil is the 'devil's excrement'.) This means increased exposure to the swings of the global commodity markets, government mismanagement of resources, the creation of hugely powerful non-governmental interests ranging from foreign oil companies to domestic oligarchs, and the engendering of weak, ineffectual, unstable or corrupt institutions.[1] In the twenty-first century the simple fact is that those countries requiring ever greater supplies of oil, with limited or non-existent domestic oil reserves of their own, are seeking supplies from all nations with reserves. This has created a world of oil haves and oil have-nots and the relationships between them have become far more complex and intertwined than at any previous point in history.

Before we discuss some of the issues directly affecting the movement of oil by sea it is necessary to appreciate fully the range of countries now seeking additional oil supplies and the places from which they are seeking them. This is no longer simply about the developed nations securing oil supplies from the Middle East; it involves many more countries sourcing oil from many more suppliers.

Oil import dependent nations are actively seeking additional supplies through exploring, drilling, mergers and acquisitions (M&A), takeovers and flattery – indeed any way they can ensure supply. As an example, let us look at just one oil company in just one oil-hungry country over just one short time period – the China National Petroleum Corporation (CNPC) and its activities between July and October 2009. CNPC operates its core business via its listed entity PetroChina and is now Asia's largest oil and gas producer.

- In July 2009 CNPC announced that it would commence deepwater oil and gas exploration after 2015 when some deepwater facilities become available. CNPC has some blocks in Africa and the Middle East, but they are still in the early stages of development.
- Just days later CNPC announced it would carry out further explorations in the South China Sea.
- In late July CNPC proposed offering US$13–14.5 bn for a controlling stake in Spanish oil giant Repsol YPF SA's Argentine unit. The transaction would be China's largest overseas takeover to date.
- In September 2009 CNPC secured a US$30 bn Chinese state loan to fund overseas expansion.
- Just days later the Venezuelan President Hugo Chávez announced that China will invest US$16 bn to boost oil production in the

country as part of a strategy to reduce dependence on the US and strengthen oil ties with other nations. Chavez had previously visited China in April 2009 to meet CNPC to seek financing for oil projects. CNPC has a minority stake in the Petrocaracol joint venture, which operates oil fields in Venezuela, and is certifying reserves in the Junin 4 area of the Orinoco belt. A newly announced joint venture between Petróleos de Venezuela SA (PDVSA) and CNPC will pump oil from Junin 4 to supply a 400,000 bpd refinery to be built in China.

- Also in September, CNPC started seeking to negotiate takeovers including PetroChina's US$1.7 bn agreement to buy 60 per cent stakes in Canada's Athabasca Oil Sands Corporation's (AOSC) MacKay River and Dover oil-sands projects in northern Alberta, and the purchase of Singapore Petroleum Corporation, the island state's only listed refinery, for US$2.2 bn.

- In October 2009 CNPC issued a statement announcing that it would boost output from oil fields overseas to more than 100 mn tonnes by 2010, accounting for more than a quarter of China's total.

- However, CNPC's bid for Canada's Verenex, whose assets are mostly in Libya, failed to get approval from the Libyan government in Tripoli, which gave a local oil firm priority (via the Libyan Investment Authority – the country's Sovereign Wealth Fund) to purchase Verenex. Another CNPC deal, to purchase the oil assets in Mangystau province, Kazakhstan, was also delayed.

CNPC is now active globally, and is well funded courtesy of the Chinese Communist Party–State, pursuing new finds, exploiting existing reserves, securing deals and agreements with companies on every continent and supported in its endeavours as a strategic operation and 'national champion' by Beijing. Some deals have worked, others have not, but CNPC is far from the only Chinese oil company engaged globally in such activities, nor is it the only Asian company – it just happens to be the largest.

The New International Web of Oil-based Relationships

As the sources of oil supply diversify across additional producing countries and territories, new high-volume oil consumers are seeking both additional sources of supply and new relationships with their existing suppliers. The global oil relationship has changed from one of Middle Eastern supply dominance and Western super consumption to one of more and new super oil consumers and more and new petro supply powers. This is leading to a growing number of traditional and new consumers chasing oil supplies around the world to ship back to their economies.

It's quite obvious why governments dream of finding oil on their territory – it's a fast track to wealth. It's equally obvious why oil-hungry nations need relations with oil-producing nations. For those countries whose oil needs have grown massively in recent decades these are often new relationships which require a tweaking of their diplomacy with established oil producers and a major effort in getting ahead of the game with the new producers. Many new producers have the oil and the willingness to sell it but often lack the technology to extract it, and this is where newly cash-rich partners such as China and India can, and do, become involved. Therefore it is instructive to look at how the rising oil-dependent nations are adjusting their relationships with the established producers first and then where and how they are seeking alternatives to Middle Eastern oil elsewhere in the world.

It has not been an easy process. Twice in the last decade China's CNPC has become embroiled in politically charged deals in Russia: a bid for a majority stake in the oil company Slavneft in 2002 led to an outcry from the Russian parliament. Slavneft, one of the top ten oil majors in Russia, recovered 16.1 mn tonnes of oil in 2002 alone. CNPC's bid was rejected and Slavneft was sold for a lower fee to domestic Russian interests. Three years later CNPC's takeover of PetroKazakhstan was only permitted to proceed after the Chinese agreed to sell one-third of the firm to a local player. It isn't just Moscow or Astana that gets nationalistic when it comes to oil-related assets. China National Offshore Oil Corporation's (CNOOC) offer in 2005 to buy the American oil company Unocal Corporation (of which more below) saw American politicians up in arms and citing security concerns. Similar problems have occurred elsewhere in the world over the attempted purchase of oil assets by China as well as by other East Asian nations and India.

More recently the strategy has been changed. Countries seeking new oil relationships, such as China and India, have sought to build longer-term relationships with resource-rich countries at a governmental level while state oil firms have turned their attention to smaller and lower-value investments that are not so likely to draw political fire. This approach has been more successful although, as arguments over Darfur, and other places where newly oil dependent nations have sought supplies shows, it is by no means a smooth process.

However, the attempt to improve and strengthen relations with the major oil-producing states of the Middle East have also been ongoing and also appear more successful and are a crucial part of both the new international web of oil-based relationships and a wider global rebalancing.

Table 3.1 **Sources of oil imports for Japan, China and India, 2008**

	To		
	Japan	China	India
From			
USA	75*	16	14
South & Central America	1	334	154
Former USSR	165	453	40
Middle East	3,960	1,844	2,167
Africa	129	1,079	435
Other	595	667	206
Total imports	**4,925**	**4,393**	**3,016**

Source: *BP Statistical Review of World Energy*, June 2009
Note: * = '000 bpd

The Resurrection of the Silk Road

It is certainly true that the latest manifestation of the rise of the Middle East oil states – Dubai's skyline is the usual accompanying photograph to illustrate this in the media – has occurred at the same time and is intrinsically linked to the rise of China and East Asia as a manufacturing region. Of course the Arab nations and peoples have been trading with China and East Asia for centuries, though the rise of China's economy, in particular, has prompted a concomitant rise in East Asian oil demand from the Middle East. Subsequently, the amount of oil leaving the UAE, Saudi Arabia, Iraq, etc. for China, East Asia and India has grown substantially. This relationship is not just about oil. Arab investments in China, from small-scale sourcers and traders to major corporations involved in hotel construction and other investments, are growing while East Asian companies have become steadily more involved in the Gulf States and throughout the Middle East.

As the economist Ben Simpfendorfer has shown, since 9/11 this closer relationship between China and the Middle East has become even more close as the Arab world's relationships with Europe and America become increasingly strained, 'China offers [*the Middle East*] an alternative strategic partner. It offers a way for the Arab world to hedge its relationship with the West. The resurrection of the Silk Road is a timely reminder that the world's centre of gravity may not always lie with the West.'[2] Since 2001 there has been a global balancing (as well as of 9/11, 2001 was also the year China joined the WTO, where they encountered a rising number of Arab oil producers around the table – seven Arab countries including the UAE and Saudi Arabia also joined the WTO between 1990 and 2005). This is a global rebalancing that has serious ramifications not just for the Middle East and East Asia but also for the West, and additionally for the issue of the movement of oil from one place to another upon which both ends of the chain rely. The wealth of Dubai (and other oil-producing states in the Middle East) relies increasingly on East Asian dependence on their oil while that wealth is increasingly spent in the glittering malls and consumer palaces that have been built across the region and are stuffed full of East Asian made goods produced in factories in turn powered by

Middle Eastern oil. The Sino-Middle Eastern relationship is growing particularly fast:

- Chinese exports to the twenty-two members of the Arab League jumped to US$62.3 bn in 2008 from just US$7.2 bn in 2001, the year China joined the WTO.
- Imports from the Arab world to China over the same period (2001–2008) shot up to US$70.3 bn from US$7.5 bn, doubling the share in total imports to 6.2 per cent, according to official Chinese data.

The record highs in oil prices in the first years of the twenty-first century significantly boosted wealth in the Arab oil-producing countries – according to the IMF, average economic growth in the Middle Eastern producing nations averaged 6 per cent between 2004 and 2007. The developed world – primarily North America, the EU and Japan – hovered at around 2.9 per cent; China of course was claiming double-digit growth throughout this period.

In those years oil prices rose by unprecedented levels – from less than US$30 a barrel to nearly US$150 a barrel between 2004 and 2008 – and a major part of the reason for that rise was the heightened demand in China and the apparent willingness of the Chinese to secure their oil needs at any price necessary. The same can be said for so many other commodities that soared in price in the same period thanks to China, most notably iron ore. Unlike in the case of iron ore, China was not the sole cause of this dramatic rise in oil prices per barrel – other East Asian countries too played their part, with growing demand, while the Western consumer, encouraged by their banks and governments, opted to enjoy a historically long and self-indulgent debt-fuelled consumption binge benefitting both the Middle Eastern oil producers and the Chinese manufacturers. The relationship between Middle Eastern oil reserves and Chinese manufacturing power has been symbiotic – after a decade of austerity in the Arab world the sharply rising oil prices prompted renewed and lavish government spending while individual households started purchasing consumer goods again, mostly imported, and mostly imported from a booming China that had factories galore but precious few oil reserves. The oil increasingly flowed East; the manufactured goods increasingly flowed West. The statistics tell the story:

1   Between 2004 and 2008 China accounted for fully one-third of the total increase in world oil consumption surpassing Japan to become the second largest gas-guzzling nation on earth in total terms after the USA. Clearly the Middle East was the biggest beneficiary in this sudden and immense thirst.

2   According to the IMF, in 2000 the Middle East's (ex-Israel) imports from China were minimal at around US$6 bn and severely lagged those of the USA (US$18 bn), Germany (US$12 bn) and the UK (US$9 bn). By 2008 things were very different and the Middle East's imports from China had rocketed up to US$48 bn – surpassing those of Germany or the UK and nudging the USA's US$50 bn.

This is rebalancing in action. Arguably the Middle East has benefitted from more goods but it is China that has the long-lasting advantage from this rebalancing and it showed in 2009. As export orders from Europe and America dropped, China's manufacturing sector suffered. But the old adage that 'if America catches a cold, China will get a severe dose of the flu' didn't hold. China had diversified its export destinations and its export products – it wasn't simply all low-end US$2 T-shirts but was everything from iPods to advanced oil rig installations while the destination of these exports were not just the developed world but everywhere – not only the Middle East but also other developing areas where China's presence, financially, culturally, militarily and in terms of aid, is being felt. 'Made in China' goods are now common in Central Asia, Russia, Latin America and, as has seemingly been of most interest to the international media, Africa.

This was not then just rebalancing but actually the new basis of the global economy and financial system – the Middle East sold oil to China; China produced goods to export; Western consumers flashed the plastic and bought them in dizzying numbers. Most people of course saw this quite clearly. What many did not see was that the Middle East's suddenly enlarged oil-derived profits were invested to support the US dollar while the new profits being made by the Chinese government from their manufacturers were being largely spent on both imports and, more importantly, US Treasury Bills (T-Bills). Both the oil producers and the Chinese became creditor nations to the American (and, to a lesser extent) the European consumer and their governments enjoying credit binges. It was perhaps rather an unholy 'Holy Trinity' for global capitalism to rest upon but mutual reliance meant that it held up. All of this can of course change and is changing. Oil revenues subsequently fell, along with prices per barrel, meaning that the Middle East's sovereign wealth funds are not the global dynamos they once were a few years ago while China's export earnings are down. Anyway, the Chinese are increasingly diversifying into a wider range of investments for their massive foreign exchange reserves – not simply American T-bills, traditionally seen as the least risky investment available, but now investments that carry greater elements of risk.

Both China's foreign exchange reserves and the Middle Eastern sovereign wealth funds are crucial lynchpins in the global economic system. China's foreign exchange reserves total US$1,400 bn. The growth of these safer investments in American debt has been staggering – from US$20 bn in the early 1990s to approximately US$450 bn by 2008. That meant that China has been the second largest global holder of American federal debt after Japan and a lynchpin in the American financial system.

The Middle Eastern sovereign wealth funds may be somewhat depleted following the crash of 2008–2009 but at their peak totalled an estimated US$1,400 bn led by the funds amassed in Kuwait, UAE and Qatar. 'Estimated' is important here – the Middle Eastern sovereign wealth funds are perhaps the most secretive significant amounts of finance in the world – they are not subject to rigorous disclosure rules and are closely connected to the ruling elites and families in the Middle East. China's notoriously murky and questionable official statistics appear open and transparent by comparison. For instance, the Abu Dhabi Investment Authority controls a fund of approximately US$800 bn, less than some major private investment funds in the West admittedly, but Abu Dhabi is just one of the seven emirates that comprise the UAE and has a native population of less than 500,000 people. Saudi Arabia is the world's largest oil producer, though its fund is only approximately US$300 bn, but has a population of approximately

28 mn people, requiring it to spend more and save less while having an enormous defence budget. Kuwait, Qatar, Oman and even Libya also have funds that run into the many billions of dollars – all largely the product of the surge in oil prices since 2004 and growing demand from both the traditional oil markets and a rising East Asia.

Most of this Middle Eastern money flowed into America through investments and was generally welcomed. However, that all changed after 9/11. America's increasingly belligerent attitude towards the Middle East, the war in Iraq of course, security restrictions against Arabs entering America all contributed to significantly frostier relations and distrust. This distrust reached a peak, and a very crucial peak for those looking at the question of oil and the high seas, in 2005 when DP World (the container ports subsidiary of Dubai World, a holding company owned by the government of Dubai), one of the world's largest port operators involved in over thirty countries, announced it was acquiring the Peninsular and Orient Steam Navigation Company (P&O). The deal would result in DP World controlling six American ports in New York, New Jersey, Philadelphia, Baltimore, New Orleans and Miami. After the deal was secured, the arrangement was reviewed by the Committee on Foreign Investment in the United States headed by the US Treasury Department and including the Departments of State, Commerce and Homeland Security. It got the green light, but soon after both Democratic and Republican members of Congress expressed concern over the potential negative impact the deal would have on port security. The American media attacked the deal while a cross-section of American politicians, including (then Senator) Hillary Clinton vocally opposed the deal. The Republican representative from North Carolina, Sue Myrick, sent a one-sentence letter to the president that read (she also posted it on her website – http://www.suemyrick. com), 'Dear Mr. President: In regard to selling American ports to the United Arab Emirates, not just No – but Hell no!'

President George W. Bush threatened to veto any legislation passed by Congress to block the DP World deal, which would have been the first time in his presidency that he had exercised the privilege. Bush claimed, 'It would send a terrible signal to friends and allies not to let this transaction go through.'[3] The UAE was friendly to America, the UAE was allowing US warships in the Persian Gulf to dock in their ports and resupply their ships with oil, food and other goods for free. Crew members were allowed shore leave in UAE member states.

DP World eventually withdrew and sold P&O's US assets to an American buyer – but the message had been understood loud and clear. Chinese politicians, business people, intellectuals and the media looked at the hostility in America to the DP World deal and drew parallels to their own recent problems with expansion as they sought to use their new-found manufacturing wealth to grow their businesses internationally and acquire oil assets. Many in China had grumbled when some in America had protested over Chinese computer company Lenovo's acquisition of IBM's personal PC business but more relevant were Chinese anger and hurt feelings over China National Offshore Oil Corporation's (CNOOC) all-cash US$18.5 bn offer in 2005 to buy American oil company Unocal Corporation, topping an earlier bid by ChevronTexaco. Understandably CNOOC saw Unocal's extensive oil interests in Central Asia as an excellent strategic fit for CNOOC. CNOOC is a Chinese state-owned oil company, 70 per cent of shares are owned by Beijing (CNOOC also has a listed arm CNOOC Ltd which trades in Hong Kong and New York and China Oilfield Services (COSL), another subsidiary, listed in Hong Kong) and part of its remit is to ensure adequate oil supplies for the PRC. Once again President Bush had appealed for a hands-off approach to the deal, but a broad group of Democrats and Republicans in Congress organised opposition to CNOOC's bid. They argued that with US$13 bn of the bid for Unocal coming from the Chinese government, the offer did not represent a free market transaction and had questionable motives. They also argued that a similarly positioned deal by a US company into China would not be allowed by Beijing and, most importantly to Sino-American relations and understanding, they argued that Chinese communist ownership of oil assets would represent a regional and economic security risk. One cry heard from the more vocal of American opponents to the deal was that through acquiring Unocal, China was moving completely to control world oil. The deal fell through and in China, as in the Middle East over the DP World deal, the lesson learned was that America was both protectionist, anti-Arab/Chinese and aggressive.

The fall-out from business debacles such as DP World/P&O and CNOOC/Unocal are not of course that the Middle East or China will cease seeking to invest in the United States – but they have found that they can invest in each other and that these investments are, by and large, free of the sort of hysteria that accompanied their planned purchases in America. The Middle East sells oil to China; China returns goods to the Middle East's consumers. Both get richer – why not continue the rebalancing and mutual benefit by investing increasingly in each other's financial markets (various Middle Eastern wealth funds are investing heavily in the Chinese stock market through the Qualified Foreign Institutional Investors – QFII – scheme that allows foreigners to invest in local stocks), construction and property industries (everything from hotels in Shanghai to apartment blocks in Tianjin) and tourism (with a noticeable uptick in direct flights between China and the Middle East)? And that is exactly what has happened – growing oil revenues to the Middle East from China are increasingly being recycled back through investments across China. And some of this investment will be related directly to oil rather than just Dubai-funded luxury hotels in Shanghai and vice versa.

For China in particular, this improved relationship with the Middle East has been vital and so far beneficial. Despite a highly active campaign by Beijing to find new sources of oil around the world to reduce dependence on the Middle East, China still sources in excess of 40 per cent of its total oil needs from the region, with nearly 22 per cent coming from Saudi Arabia (approximately 0.5 million bpd) and nearly 15 per cent from Iran alone while Oman, Kuwait, the UAE and Yemen were also among China's ten biggest suppliers. The Middle East will remain crucial. As Ben Simpfendorfer has noted, 'Even if they [*China*] were buying everything that either Angola or Kazakhstan had to sell, they would still only be supplying a quarter of what they need. Inevitably they have to go back to the Middle East.'[4] But in the Middle East, China will still be competing for oil with the established Western oil giants such as ExxonMobil, Shell and BP, who have long-term relationships with many regional governments often backed up by stronger diplomatic ties and military treaties of protection between their home countries and Middle Eastern governments. China, and the other oil-hungry nations of East Asia, will source more from the Middle East in the coming decades but it seems unlikely they will come to dominate or dislodge the major Western oil companies.

Therefore, they have had to look further afield and in more diverse locations for oil.

Scouring the Globe for Black Gold

The new competition for oil globally by the new super consumers such as China and India is not a primary subject of this book. However, a quick overview of where countries are now seeking oil is important as it indicates the plurality of destinations from which oil is being shipped to Asia, which impacts on more germane discussions about the future of the shipment of oil through the world's SLOCs, the rise of piracy in various areas and other factors. Two major regions of new supply are particularly important here: Latin America and Africa.

East Asia's interest in diversifying its oil imports away from being overly reliant on the Middle East really took off around 2004 when world oil prices began to rise sharply. The region, and especially China, had already become concerned about stability in the area with the invasion of Iraq, and growing tensions between America and Iran, as well as rising prices, merely confirmed the belief that alternative sources needed to be found, deals needed to be done, money needed to be invested and supplies needed to be secured as swiftly as possible. In 2004 and 2005 China, as well as other East Asian oil dependent nations signed a raft of accords with Venezuela, as well investing in largely untapped markets such as Peru and exploring possibilities in Bolivia, Colombia and other Latin American energy markets.

For China, Venezuela has been a key new supplier and diplomatic and business partner. There's a confluence of interest between the two countries – China seeking to diversify its energy supplies; Venezuela seeking to diversify its energy business beyond the United States (which in 2005 took in excess of 60 per cent of Venezuela's crude oil). And the relationship has blossomed – in January 2005 the Venezuelan President, Hugo Chávez and China's Vice-President Zeng Qinghong signed nineteen cooperation agreements in Caracas including long-range plans for Chinese stakes in oil and gas fields. Further agreements have followed. Given that the United States is only a relatively short tanker trip from Venezuela, it seems likely that

America will continue to take most of the country's supplies, but diversification is occurring.

In July 2009 Hugo Chávez announced that he had three strategic energy objectives as regards China: 1) for Chinese oil companies working in Venezuela to boost their oil output and supply China to one million barrels a day by 2013; 2) to review the status of a planned joint venture oil refinery to be built in China; and 3) to create a bilateral Venezuela-PRC oil shipping company.[5] By September 2009 the first objective was achieved with the signing of a US$16 bn investment deal to last three years and cover a joint venture between the Chinese and Venezuela's state-owned PDVSA to produce 450,000 bpd of extra heavy crude in the Orinoco basin. This followed a similar US$20 bn deal with Russian oil firms (Rosneft, Lukoil, Gazprom, TNK-BP and Surgutneftegaz) working in the same Orinoco oil belt expected to produce 450,000 bpd by 2012.[6]

Chávez's second objective – an oil refinery – is also getting closer. PetroChina and Venezuela have announced that they will build a refinery in Guangdong Province that will equal China's largest existing oil-processing plant in terms of capacity. A joint shipping line has not yet been created but talks continue.

China is not the only oil dependent East Asian nation interested in Venezuela. Chávez and Japan's then Prime Minister Taro Aso agreed to cooperate on oil and gas developments in June 2009, forming a joint committee to study financing development and exploration in the Orinoco basin. Venezuela is expected to continue to explore new deals with East Asia and other countries following Chavez's ongoing fractious relationship with Washington and the declines in oil prices that have forced him to cut government spending.

Other Latin American countries are also receiving an increasing number of delegations from Asian businessmen and politicians. Often deals are linked to development and lending. Ecuador's President Rafael Correa has signed such an agreement with Beijing commenting that, 'China has offered us initial capital worth one billion dollars for infrastructure projects, we are going to pay little by little with our oil.'[7] China has indeed loaned money to Quito (the smallest member of OPEC) and the Ecuadorian government will repay the loan in the medium and long term with crude oil supplies. Additionally, Brazil's state-controlled Petroleo Brasileiro SA (Petrobras) has received US$10 bn in loans from Beijing to develop the country's largest crude discovery in over thirty years which aims to supply 150,000 bpd to China in 2009 rising to 200,000 bpd in 2010.

Such deals continue between China and other East Asian nations across Latin America, but it is oil-related agreements and contracts in Africa that have raised more concerns in recent years.

African Excursion

The oil-hungry nations of East Asia seeking new suppliers and armed with 'no strings' money to invest have become key players in the emerging African oil industry across the continent from the Sahara to the Cape. The Chinese government, especially after the country's economy started booming, has been liberal in offering credit and aid on generous terms to oil-producing African nations. By some counts China now sources 25–30 per cent of its oil imports from the African continent. In 2009 alone, China took 30 per cent of Angola's total oil exports and 60 per cent of Sudan's output.

Africa is seen as one major answer to East Asia's oil dependency dilemma. Companies can seemingly acquire equity stakes in African oil assets and become deeply and personally involved in African oil extraction in a way impossible in the Middle East. China has certainly courted the African oil nations heavily – over US$20 bn of aid and concessionary financing to various African governments recently, as well as high-profile visits, delegations and summits in Beijing. Chinese Premier Hu Jintao visited Africa three times in three years, a major effort for a leader who is reported intensely to dislike travel. In February 2006 Angola briefly overtook Saudi Arabia as China's major oil supplier. All looked set for expansion – China's oil refining industry is mostly geared to handle sweet crude (with a low sulphur content) which favours African oil over Saudi Arabian (a mix of sweet and sour crude). However, (with Saudi Arabian help and finance in some cases) China built refineries capable of dealing with Saudi sour crude. Nevertheless, Africa remains important but also contentious for media-shy Beijing.

Since China has seriously started to seek oil supply deals in Africa (again around 2004 and the rises in global oil prices) Beijing has taken what it sees as a highly pragmatic approach, stressing business and development and keen to emphasise that it was not a former colonial power but a friend of the region. It is a strategy that has largely worked, despite criticism that China has unfairly used diplomatic leverage, ignored corruption and conflicts, done nothing to encourage transparency in the industry and little to create jobs in the countries in which it invests. Beijing counters that Europeans and Americans take more oil from Africa than China does, have done so for decades (through both imperialism and business) and have hardly left a shining legacy. The debate will continue and need not concern us here – what is important is that China is sourcing more oil from more African countries and so having to ship additional amounts from the continent to China.

Of course the Western nations too are looking to secure their existing oil supply arrangements and find new ones. Britain's new and oft criticised relationship with Libya, and France's with various francophone African nations, are just two examples that show how fractious and divisive the quest for oil supplies can be in any country. But it has often been the efforts of the new oil super consumers to diversify their supply chains that have grabbed the headlines, as this seems to many to be symptomatic of the new global rebalancing of the world's oil economy, and in turn the wider international economy. If there is one area of the movement of oil supplies by sea in which it seems the traditional oil dependent economies of the West and the newly oil dependent economies of East Asia are facing the same threat then it is the question of the management of the world's SLOCs and by extension the specific problem of the dramatic rise in piracy in some of the world's busiest and most important sea lanes in recent years – the subject of the next two chapters.

CHAPTER FOUR

Securing the SLOCs

Wednesday 22 July 2009 – Breakfast at the Grand Hotel Europe, St Petersburg

Occasionally, just occasionally, the life of a jobbing freelance journalist offers luxurious treats.

The sonorous melodies of the harp resonate around the gilded, stunning room at the heart of the historic Grand Hotel Europe. In front are a mound of strawberries and three bottles of champagne on ice. Traversing to the centre of the decorated hall, gazing up at the ornate stained window ceiling and the beautiful lighting, there's a pile of caviar waiting to be wolfed down. This is elegant luxury defined. It also happens to be breakfast for a couple of glorious days in wonderful St Petersburg. Whoever came up with the dietary mantra that one should eat breakfast like a king, lunch like a prince and dinner like a pauper may well have had this Tsar-tastic brekkie in mind.

Eggs Benedict served, espresso to his side, the Russian oilman opposite opens up about what he terms as 'the new energy frontier'. Keen not to be identified for fear of annoying the powers that be in Moscow, the well-placed executive says, 'Up north is where you'll see the most exciting oil and gas developments in the coming years,' referring to the Barents Sea around the Arctic Circle. Taking a slurp from his freshly squeezed orange juice, he recounts how he's just returned from Murmansk, the ice-free port at the north-western edge of the Russian realm, close to Finland. 'Everyone there says the Arctic will become more and more open to commercial shipping. We Russians have to make sure we are on top of opportunities there.'

65

Indeed, as he is speaking, two German ships are preparing a groundbreaking – or icebreaking – voyage through the Arctic North East Passage from Asia to Europe, a route that the ships' owners claim saves 3,000 miles over the more traditional Indian Ocean route. Once this was just a dream; every year it becomes more of a reality.

Russia's oil reserves stand at 80 bn barrels. Importantly, oil majors, including the man now picking up his knife and fork here, reckon there's 100 bn more barrels to find – 'the biggest exploration prize in the world', in the words of Robert Dudley, the former boss of TNK-BP, BP's Russian joint venture. Much of this new-found energy is coming from the icy waters around the Arctic Circle.

Stabbing his eggs, the bright yolk seeping out onto his plate, the high placed oilman outlines Russia's first Arctic oil and gas endeavours, something he's intimately connected to. Gazprom, the country's largest energy company, is developing Shtokman in the icy waters of the Barents Sea 400 miles north-east of Murmansk, together with France's Total and Norway's StatoilHydro. Gazprom is also developing the Prirazlomnoye oil field in the Pechora Sea to the east.

'These two are just the tip of the iceberg,' he says, smiling at his own heavily accented joke. 'The Arctic will increasingly be a source of international friction. We, as Russians, must protect our rights to this resource-rich region.'

Denmark (via its control of Greenland), Canada, Sweden, Norway, Finland, the USA and Canada are all just as keen to have a confirmed slice of this area. Global warming has made the Arctic a hot topic and a new energy frontier with many nations suddenly deploying navies to the far north to enforce their territorial claims.

Sailors have been trying to forge a way through the Arctic connecting Europe and Asia for hundreds of years. Rising temperatures will ensure the region becomes the latest controversial vital sea lane of communication.

'We (Russia) have sovereignty. Now we must enforce it,' says the burly man opposite, gulping down the dregs of his espresso. With that he stands to leave. He's off to inspect an icebreaker under construction nearby.

Addiction Requires a Reliable Supply

Since man first worked out that wood floated and built a raft, the importance of safe and secure sea trade and communications has been a paramount national security requirement. Naval dominance has consistently been the best way to flaunt a country's rising power. Since the Ancient Greeks, with their swift, sleek brass-bowed triremes that dramatically overcame the Persians at the Battle of Salamis in 480 BC, beating a navy three times larger than their own, world power has been cemented by ocean control.

Fast forward 1,300-odd years and the British Empire was founded on the back of the daring-do verging-on-piratical acts of Elizabethan swashbucklers such as Sir Walter Raleigh. Repelling the Spanish Armada gave the nation the confidence to explore further afield and marked the slide of the Spanish Empire.

Global marine priorities changed with the advent of large-scale oil production in the late nineteenth century. The world's most developed nations rapidly became hooked on oil for their daily lives. Maintaining economic prosperity meant securing reliable sources of oil.

Take World War II as a classic example. Hitler's Operation Barbarossa had oil gains around Baku as a strategic priority for the fateful decision to go to war with the USSR. At his birthday before the Soviet invasion Hitler was presented with a cake with a neat icing map of the Caspian Sea and the letters B-A-K-U spelled out in chocolate cream. After eating the cake, Hitler said: 'Unless we get Baku oil, the war is lost.'[1] He wasn't wrong. Hitler's urgent oil requirements opened up the Eastern Front, the single largest battlefront in the history of mankind. Ultimately, this was the decision that cost the Nazi regime its existence. Likewise, Allied and Axis military decisions in North Africa were taken with oil supplies very much in mind.

Eleven years after the war when Egypt's dictator Gamal Adbel Nasser took over and nationalised the Suez Canal, the European powers of Paris and London, realising that the smooth flow of oil imports was under threat, were quick to rush into military action. 'No arrangements for the future of this great international waterway could be acceptable to Her Majesty's Government which would leave it in the unfettered control of a single power which could, as recent events have shown, exploit it purely for purposes of national policy,' then British Prime Minister Sir Anthony Eden told the House of Commons in 1956, ahead of one last imperial folly as the Suez crisis unfolded that summer.[2]

Controlling the sea lanes is still to control the world.

Box 4.1 Suez: Bringing Continents Together

The desire for a waterway to link Europe and Asia has been around for a very long time. As early as the Egyptian Twelfth Dynasty, Pharaoh Senusret III (1878–1839 BC) may have had a west–east canal dug through the Wadi Tumilat, joining the Nile with the Red Sea. At the end of the eighteenth century, Napoleon Bonaparte, while in Egypt, contemplated the construction of a channel to join the Mediterranean and Red Sea. More than sixty years on, the Frenchman Ferdinand Marie de Lesseps was the visionary who would eventually link continents. He was a career diplomat and his close diplomatic ties with the ruling elite in Egypt paid off with a contract to build the Suez Canal. Investors came in from all over the globe, although the project found detractors, among them the great railway engineer, Robert Stephenson, who predicted that the proposed canal would fill with sludge. The canal's opening in 1869, after eleven years' hard work, and its success thereafter proved the critics wrong. Aged seventy-four, de Lesseps embarked on his next great project – the Panama Canal. It was to beat him in its complexity and tough terrain, leaving the Americans to finish that continent-cutting construction.

The Suez Canal (which has no locks as there is no difference in water level along its length) opened to traffic on 17 November 1869. It had an immediate and dramatic effect on world trade. Thanks to its construction and the completion of the American Transcontinental Railroad six months earlier, the entire world could be circled in record time (and Jules Verne's Phileas Fogg could go *Around the World in Eighty Days* in 1872). But the Suez Canal quickly became a new and key chokepoint for world trade – a man-made

---

and vulnerable SLOC. Closure of the 120-mile Suez Canal and the nearby Sumed Pipeline would add 6,000 miles of transit around the continent of Africa.

Nowadays, more than 3,000 oil tankers pass through the Suez Canal annually, and represent around 25 per cent of the Canal's total revenues (which totalled US$4.74 bn for the 2008–2009 fiscal year). Only 1,000 feet at its narrowest point, the Canal is unable to handle very large tankers. However, the Cairo state-owned Suez Canal Authority has recently embarked on a widening and deepening scheme to accommodate VLCCs, which will boost traffic and revenues for the Canal Authority.

Fig. 4.1 A tanker queuing to transit the Suez Canal

The US Takes Control of the High Seas

At the end of World War II the United States was already by far the world's largest consumer of oil. Up until then coal had been the pre-eminent raw material for electricity supply. However, scientists had worked hard during the war on understanding the full industrial possibilities of oil and petrochemicals. It soon became clear that oil in its myriad forms could be used for thousands of divergent products from fertilisers to food additives. King Coal's reign in the contemporary world's fastest-growing economy was coming to an end. In future the issue of oil in Washington DC would become intertwined with both foreign and military policy.

America's domestic consumption of petrol grew from 22.3 bn gallons in 1945 to 63.7 bn in 1960 – a growth of nearly 35 per cent. Before the war the US was self-sufficient in crude oil production. The horizon-to-horizon scenes of gushers in the arid Texas outback led many to believe the US had indefinite reserves of 'black gold'. Indeed, even in 1945 America was able to export 4 per cent of its supply overseas. However, within five years 10 per cent of domestic oil consumption was being imported from abroad to make up the shortfall. In the 1950s petroleum imports leapt from 592 mn barrels to 1.54 bn barrels per annum – a steep upward trend that would continue unabated until the Oil Crisis of the 1970s. By 1970 the US was importing fully one-third of its supply and as much as one-half by 1980. That figure now stands at 62 per cent.

America had moved early to extend its influence internationally in the oil business. Before World War II the US controlled most of Venezuela's oil supplies but just 13 per cent of that of the Middle East, a region where the Americans were slow to follow the British lead. With the withdrawal of the British as a colonial power from the region, America was quick to step up its interests. By 1959 American firms controlled 64 per cent of the Middle East's reserves. Safe access to the increasingly congested Suez Canal became vital for the continued growth of oil-addicted America. Combine this growing overseas oil dependency with the rise of communism in the Asia-Pacific region and the heightening of the Cold War, and the scene was set for America's firm presence in the Pacific arena throughout the second half of the twentieth century.

It is hard to imagine now, but prior to America's entry into World War I and its later adoption of the role of the world's policeman, the US was very much an introverted place with little ambition or volition to look outside its own borders. Non-interventionism and isolationism had been the norm, as set down in stone in George Washington's farewell address, where he noted: 'The great rule of conduct for us, in regard to domestic nations, is in extending our commercial relations, to have with them as little political connection as possible.'³ In the 1890s there was some bubbling of Pacific intent with the takeover of Hawaii. The Spanish–American War of 1898 was a blip in the non-interventionist policy, forced upon America by the nearness of the enemy, just 90 miles from the mainland of America in Cuba – 'America's backyard'. This skirmish gave the US its first key foothold in the Pacific in the form of the former Spanish colony, the Philippines, named after Phillip II in Madrid. However, it was President Woodrow Wilson, who had just won re-election with the campaign slogan 'He kept us out of the war,' who sent troops to the trenches of France in 1917 and brought America firmly onto the international stage.

Despite attempts to return to its insular self in the intervening period, the invasion of Pearl Harbor in December 1941 brought the US back into the global arena. Ironically, the US had actually practised war games with Japan in mind as early as the 1920s. Britain's naval power was on the wane. The Anglo–Japanese Naval Agreement of 1902 gave the Japanese the rights to patrol the seaways of the Pacific, leaving Britain's Royal Navy to focus its stretched resources elsewhere.

The sensational sinking of the battleship *HMS Prince of Wales* and the battle cruiser *HMS Repulse* in December 1941 by Japanese aircraft off Singapore effectively ended all British marine presence in the region and spurred the US, hit hard by Pearl Harbor, to ramp up its Pacific presence. Sir Winston Churchill would write later of his dismay of the double sinking:

> In all the war, I never received a more direct shock ... As I turned over and twisted in bed the full horror of the news sank in upon me. There were no British or American ships in the Indian Ocean or the Pacific except the American survivors of Pearl Harbor, who were hastening back to California. Over all this vast expanse of waters Japan was supreme, and we everywhere were weak and naked.⁴

By the end of the war the US had established a strong presence around the Pacific, one that would grow to a noose around soon-to-be communist China and Ho Chi Minh-led Vietnam. With huge forces in Japan and the

---

Box 4.2   Bosporus and Panama

Increased oil exports from the Caspian Sea region make the Bosporus Straits one of the busiest and most dangerous chokepoints in the world, supplying Western and Southern Europe with 2.4 mn bpd. The Bosporus and the Dardanelles comprise the Turkish Straits and divide Asia from Europe. The Bosporus connects the Black Sea with the Sea of Marmara, and the Dardanelles links the Sea of Marmara with the Aegean and Mediterranean Seas. The 17-mile-long waterway located in Turkey supplies Western and Southern Europe with oil from the Caspian Sea region. Traffic through the straits is expected to increase as Azerbaijan and Kazakhstan augment their crude production and exports in the future.

Only half a mile wide at its narrowest point, the Turkish Straits are one of the world's most difficult waterways to navigate due to their sinuous geography. With 50,000 vessels, including 5,500 oil tankers, passing through the straits annually, it is also one of the world's busiest. While there are no current alternative routes for westward shipments from the Black Sea and Caspian Sea region, there are several pipeline projects in various phases of development under way.

Philippines, a few in Korea, Taiwan and Thailand plus de facto owned territories in Guam, American Samoa and the Marshall Islands, the US was well positioned to rule the seas west of San Francisco and east of Singapore. Troop numbers would escalate in the Pacific twice more with the wars on the Korean peninsula in the early 1950s and then in the long-drawn-out conflict in Vietnam in the 1960s and 1970s.

However, as America's oil dependence became more acute, a holding in the Indian Ocean became important. Britain obliged, ceding the tiny island of Diego Garcia to the Pentagon on an indefinite lease in 1965. US maritime hegemony was seemingly complete from the Pacific to the North Atlantic, and with the demise of the Soviet Union became effectively global. It would be a group of pirates in the twenty-first century, rather than any nation state, that would prove no single navy – even one with twenty aircraft carriers – can patrol all the world's seas.

> While the Bosporus is primarily a tanker channel, the most famous shipping channel in the western hemisphere, the Panama Canal, actually has fairly minimal tanker exposure, with just a relatively insignificant 0.5 mn bpd shifting through its fourteen locks.
>
> The canal is 50 miles long, and only 110 feet wide at its narrowest point – Culebra Cut on the Continental Divide. Around 14,000 vessels transit the canal annually, of which around half account for traffic to and from the USA. A US$5 bn project is now under way to expand the canal. The expansion will add a third lane of traffic that will handle wider loads and new locks that will be 150 feet wide as well as deeper, and wider access canals that will allow for larger modern ships to pass. This expansion is expected to increase the total transit volume and almost double the current maximum size of ships able to use the canal. The plan is to be financed, in part, by raising current tolls through the canal; the rest will come from foreign credits.
>
> As is the case for all important thoroughfares, closure of the Panama Canal would greatly increase transit times and costs, adding over 8,000 miles of travel. Vessels would have to reroute around the Straits of Magellan, Cape Horn and Drake Passage over the tip of South America.

China's Harmonious Rise and the 'Malacca Dilemma'

Nominally, communist China has lately taken a different path to secure its own oceanic ambitions, namely splashing out lots of cash in lieu of having a world-class navy, very much in line with its avowed intentions of a 'peaceful rise' and 'harmonious society', two of the Communist Party's current slogans. The whole economy of East Asia is increasingly at the mercy of a small strip of sea, just 8,000 feet wide at its narrowest point. Eighty per cent of all of Japan and South Korea's oil comes through the Malacca Straits,[5] separating Indonesia and Malaysia, with Singapore located at its southern tip. The Malacca Straits are the busiest stretch of waterway in the world. They are also infested by pirates (see chapter 6, 'Piracy: The Nebulous Threat'). China's recent interest in the area has only really taken off in the last sixteen years. Following the 1989

73

Tiananmen Square massacre and the complicit deal struck between the ruling Communist Party and the populace, promising extreme material growth in exchange for power, the Chinese economy took off.

Up until 1993 China's oil production was sufficient to meet domestic demands. After that, securing oil from overseas became a top national security initiative. It is noticeable, for instance, that the first time the People's Republic ever laid claim to a contentious territory (apart from long-held simmering disputes over land border demarcations with Vietnam and India) was in early 1995, some fourteen months after it became a net oil importer. China caused concern by occupying Mischief Reef, long claimed by the Philippines and known in Filipino as Panganiban Reef, situated 150 miles west of the island of Palawan, the nearest Philippine landmass and some 620 miles from the Chinese coastline. In the past decade China has also put more impetus behind its claims to the disputed Spratly Islands (a group of more than 650 reefs, islets, atolls and islands in the South China Sea between the Philippines, China, Malaysia and Vietnam) as a way of edging its sphere of influence further south, thus bringing it closer to having a voice on Malacca Strait-related security matters.

By 2008 half of China's oil consumption was reliant on imports, with more than 60 per cent of these imports passing through the Malacca Straits, a figure some analysts maintain will rise to as much as 80 per cent by 2015. Furthermore, approximately a quarter of all Chinese exports transit the Malacca Straits en route to the Gulf and Europe. The infamous unspoken pact the Communist Party has made with its people in China regarding prosperity rests, then, on the continued smooth flow of oil through this tight, densely packed and often pirate-infested strip of water –what the Chinese President Hu Jintao referred to in 2003 as the 'Malacca Dilemma'.[6]

The Communist Party-controlled *China Youth Daily* wrote in June 2004: 'It is no exaggeration to say that whoever controls the Straits of Malacca will also have a stranglehold on the energy route of China.'[7] By using the Malacca Straits instead of detouring south of Indonesia, ships transiting from Europe and the Middle East to the Far East can save up to 1,000 miles, or the equivalent of three days' sailing time. Malaysia has proposed limiting the number of vessels that can enter the Straits amid worries that rising congestion could spark accidents. More than 70,000 vessels passed through the Malacca Straits in 2009, a sharp increase from about 44,000 in 1999. The Malaysian Deputy Prime Minister Najib Razak commented in October 2008, 'Malaysia believes there is an ultimate tipping point for maritime transit in the Straits, beyond which further increases would become not only risky but also too dangerous and costly.'[8] Some researchers estimate that 120,000 vessels might use the 630-mile long channel annually by 2015 if curbs are not introduced.

Into the Indian Ocean

Aware of its Achilles heel in South East Asia along the Malacca Straits and its growing volumes of oil imported from the Middle East, Beijing has been looking at alternative transport solutions since the mid-1990s. The needs of one ally-neighbour, Pakistan, and the invasion by the US of another neighbour, Afghanistan, conspired to speed up China's current Indian Ocean foray.

Pakistan had been humiliated time and time again by the vastly superior Indian Navy, most recently in 1999 when the port of Karachi, the nation's key trading artery, was blockaded. Karachi was Pakistan's main port and the blockade hurt. Its draft limitations, however, combined with its proximity to India were far from ideal and its days as a major port capable of serving larger vessels are numbered. A dusty obscure fishing village called Gwadar, far away in Pakistan's western province of Baluchistan, bordering Afghanistan to the north-west and Iran to the south-west, was subsequently earmarked for development. Strategically, its location was ideal, with the Persian Gulf to the west and the Gulf of Oman to the south-west. Its development into a deepwater multipurpose 'megaport' would require hundreds of millions of dollars that Pakistan's then President General Pervez Musharaff simply did not have. What he did have were friendly ties with his neighbour and ally China, which was only too happy to help out. An 'energy corridor' was proposed that would allow China to avoid all its normal energy chokepoints bar the Straits of Hormuz.

The Straits of Hormuz are by far the world's most important chokepoint, with an oil flow of 16.5–17 mn bpd, according to the IEA. To put that in perspective, one-fifth of all oil produced worldwide moves through this narrow maritime hook on a daily basis. Located between Oman and Iran, the Straits of Hormuz connect the Persian Gulf with the Gulf of Oman and the Arabian Sea. At its narrowest point the Straits are just 21 miles wide.

Beijing invested US$198 mn in Gwadar's first-phase development and dispatched the China Harbour Engineering Company to start construction. Beijing then also spent another US$200 mn on a coastal highway connecting remote Gwadar with Karachi. Further, China promised to spend US$526 mn on the nine-berth second phase of development at Gwadar. Pakistan in turn is attempting to build decent overland routes into Afghanistan, while Pakistan and China have both committed to upgrading the Karakoram Highway, the highest paved international road in the world that straddles both countries in mountainous terrain. The Chinese media at the time speculated whether a pipeline might accompany the upgraded highway in the future. As the port construction kicked off, Islamabad and Beijing upped the ante by joining forces to transform Gwadar into a huge oil-receiving hub. The plan called for the Chinese to build a refinery and petrochemical complex with an initial 10 mn tonnes per year (or 200,000 bpd) capacity, later expanding to 21 mn tonnes. Pakistan has allocated 5,000 hectares of land for the proposed oil city. Were all these objectives to come off, then China, via its north-western region of Xinjiang, would have overland routes all the way to Central Asia plus the possibility of importing and exporting to and from Gwadar.

However, the Chinese have learnt that projects in Pakistan do not march at the same speed as similar infrastructure developments back home. Gwadar was never going to be easy. There are those in Baluchistan province who have separatist ambitions and a low level of insurgency continues to simmer, which is made all the more unstable by its proximity to Afghanistan. While both the port and the coastal highway did open, albeit late, in the latter days of General Musharraf's presidency in 2007, after his departure further development of this strategic hub stalled. More than a year later and Federal Minister for Port and Shipping Qamaruzzaman Kaira promised a probe into the mishandling of the port: 'Deplorably, Gwadar Port is a mishandled issue as it is still lacking the connectivity network ... there is no electricity there, rail route, roads nothing,' Kaira has said.[9] The minister suggested

Fig. 4.2 Gwadar Port (Pakistan) under construction

that the port would not be fully operational before the year 2011 at the earliest. There have been other problems too. Reports have emerged of some Chinese workers receiving rough treatment from the locals. Three Chinese nationals were killed in the area in 2004. Despite government intimations that the port would be fast tracked and continuing support for the project from the post-Musharraf government, Gwadar remains stalled.

Over at the port itself, meanwhile, the Pakistan Navy's reluctance to vacate 1,400 acres of land necessary to meet the requirements stipulated with the international container terminal operator is making intermodal progress nigh on impossible. In July 2009 the impasse led Pakistan's current Ports and Shipping Minister Babar Khan Ghauri to threaten to shut down the port if the navy did not vacate the land. Exasperated by what they see as interminable lethargy and incompetence, the Chinese informed Islamabad in August 2009 that they were shelving the multi-billion-dollar oil refinery project at Gwadar. The decision, which follows the January 2009 suspension of work by the UAE state-run International Petroleum Investment Company (IPIC) on the US$5 bn Khalifa Coastal Refinery (KCR) project at Hub, also in Baluchistan, casts into doubt the future of the planned US$12.5 bn mega oil city project in Gwadar, of which the refinery there was to be a key element. China's involvement with Gwadar now looks to be on the back burner. It has invested too much to turn its back on it outright, but now appears to be waiting for signs of goals being met before handing over more cash.

The Chinese have other options in the Indian Ocean. Down in Sri Lanka the same China Harbour Engineering Company is busy building a huge port complex to the south of the island at the once sleepy fishing town of Hambantota. The giant facility will house a container terminal, as well as ultimately a refuelling and docking station for the Chinese People's Liberation Navy, helping to protect its Middle East oil. The port, signed off in March 2007, is estimated to cost US$1 bn and the Chinese are shouldering fully 85 per cent of the costs.

At around the same time as the Hambantota port deal was struck, Chinese armaments shipments to the island leapt, finally helping to kill off in bloody fashion the threat of the insurgent Tamil Tigers at the other end of the island. Although China was already Sri Lanka's biggest arms supplier in the 1990s, its arms sales to Colombo have increased significantly since 2007, when the US suspended military aid over human rights issues. 'China's arms sales have been the decisive factor in ending the military stalemate,' Brahma Chellaney of the Centre for Policy Research in New Delhi has commented, adding, 'There seems to have been a deal linked to Hambantota.'[10] The first stage of the Hambantota port project, including a 1,000-foot-long bunkering terminal, is scheduled for completion by the end of 2010.

Although China says that Hambantota is a purely commercial venture, many US and Indian military planners regard it as part of what is termed China's 'string of pearls' strategy (a Pentagon-coined term) under which China is also building or upgrading ports at Gwadar, Chittagong in Bangladesh and Sittwe in Burma. Beijing is certainly nervous about the project's details – China's internet censors blocked access to virtually all international references (at least those they could find) to Hambantota in 2009.

Christopher J. Pehrson, author of the paper for the Strategic Studies Institute (otherwise known as the US Army War College) *String of Pearls: Meeting the Challenge of China's Rising Power Across the*

Asian Littoral,[11] maintains that the 'String of Pearls' describes the manifestation of China's rising geopolitical influence through efforts to increase access to ports and airfields, develop special diplomatic relationships and modernise military forces that extend from the South China Sea through the Straits of Malacca, across the Indian Ocean and on to the Arabian Gulf.

In Bangladesh the now familiar China Harbour Engineering Company is busy at work developing a container terminal at Chittagong, just as it has done in Gwadar and Hambantota. Like Sri Lanka and Pakistan, China has ratcheted up its arms sales to Dhaka in the past decade. Some Indian observers are concerned that Dhaka may allow Chinese naval vessels to call at Chittagong. The Chinese government is pumping money into developing the 560-mile Kunming Highway which will link Chittagong to Kunming in south-west China's landlocked Yunnan province via Burma and provide yet another potential alternative to the Malacca Straits. Moreover, long overlooked river arteries from Yunnan to Bangladesh are now being dredged with a view to shifting oil by barge from Chittagong.

However, it is Bangladesh's neighbour where China's strongest alternative to the Malacca Straits lies. The secretive dictatorship that rules South East Asia's backwater of Burma has long looked to China for both cash and legitimacy. In return China has used Burma almost like a colony, employing the cheap labour there to manufacture goods and taking advantage of its geography to further Beijing's energy security. The Chinese have long had an important naval base on the Burmese coast. Now a huge gas pipeline is beginning to make its way from the coast on the Andaman Sea through the humid jungle and the mountains on the border between Burma and China that will profoundly change global energy patterns.

There has been speculation that the Chinese would use the existing Burmese port of Sittwe, closer to Bangladesh and founded by the British in the nineteenth century, for both the proposed oil and the gas pipelines. The *Myanmar Times* has commented, 'there are two reasons why the Chinese prefer the tiny port town of Kyauk Phyu [*for the oil pipeline*], about 112 km farther south: security and isolation. The island is remote with virtually no transport infrastructure linked to it. The only way to get there is by ship or by plane using a small airstrip.'[12] Similarly, China is also interested in a Malaysian pipeline and a refinery project estimated to cost approximately US$14.3 bn. This 200-mile west–east pipeline near Malaysia's troublesome border with southern Thailand would have the capacity to transfer 800,000 bpd while the planned refinery would have a capacity to process 200,000 bpd.

Finally, China has also been working hard to improve ties and navigation with all its Mekong River neighbours. This has seen oil

---

Box 4.3   A Fantasy that Might Become a Reality: The Kra Canal

The most fanciful proposal thus far for a new way to bypass the crowded and sometimes troublesome SLOCs of South East Asia has been to construct a canal across the Kra Isthmus in southern Thailand. The idea of an 'Asian Panama Canal' linking the Andaman Sea with the Gulf of Thailand, and hence the Indian and Pacific Oceans, has been around for centuries. First suggested in 1677, the proposal has been revisited at least a dozen times since then. Yet on each occasion the project has been shelved due to lack of financial resources, technical difficulties and security problems.

The idea was most recently revisited in 2001. Proponents envisaged a two-lane canal, an east–west highway running parallel, and harbours, oil refineries and storage facilities at each end. The canal, it was argued, would create jobs, generate revenue in the form of transit fees and oil refining, and benefit the global economy because ships could save three to four days' sailing time by avoiding the congested and pirate-prone Malacca Straits. Ultimately the huge cost and environmental damage this peninsula-cutting construction would bring shot down this latest revival of the Kra dream, good news for Singapore whose whole raison d'être is built around its strategic location, something that would be destroyed were the Kra ever to see the light of day. Still, there are those who seek to resurrect the project.

---

start to move by river from Thailand to Jinghong in the southern portion of China's Yunnan province. The oil transport route is a result of an agreement signed in March 2006 by China, Laos, Burma and Thailand to cooperate on the shipping of oil along the Mekong River, which connects Yunnan with the three South East Asian countries as well as Vietnam and Cambodia. Ultimately, post significant dredging, China is expecting to receive 200,000 tonnes of refined oil via the new Mekong route.

African Safari

China's advance into Africa is well documented and commented on in chapter 3. However, some details of China's involvement in port development and SLOC protection are worth considering. Trading infrastructure and cash for minerals and oil, China has made more inroads into the continent than any other nation over the last fifteen years. Bilateral trade has quintupled, to US$55 bn from 2000 to 2006, a figure that is likely to crack US$100 bn in 2010.

There are now about 750,000 Chinese living and working in Africa,[13] with pipelines fanning out in a spider's web to brand new Chinese-built oil terminals up and down the coastline. Once again the busy China Harbour Engineering Company is to the fore. Its latest deal on the continent is to build a terminal for the Suez Canal Container Terminal (SCCT) in Cairo to go alongside another recently concluded Egyptian deal to dredge Damietta Port, approximately 5 miles to the west of the Damietta branch of the River Nile in the Mediterranean Sea.

The Chinese Harbour Construction Company has also been building a port in the northern Lebanese city of Tripoli (not to be confused with the Libyan capital). After the first Israeli air strikes on Beirut Airport in July 2006, the Chinese employees working on the project remained in Lebanon. However, Israeli fighter jets then attacked a project managed by the Chinese Irrigation and Hydroelectric Company, making a Chinese project a target. Chinese workers were evacuated in vans bearing the PRC flag to warn Israeli pilots. The convoy of Chinese workers from Tripoli, the irrigation

---

Box 4.4   A New SLOC? Awakening the Arctic

Far to the north a combination of global warming and oil and
gas developments mean ships can now move through the Arctic
in summer – Germany's Beluga Shipping was the first foreign
company to do so in the summer of 2009. Year-round sea ice is fast
disappearing; this once permanent ice pack has thinned more than
1 1/2 feet in the last four years. In the same period, more than 1 mn
square miles of ice, an area about the size of Alaska, have vanished.
The Arctic seems destined to resemble the Great Lakes – frozen
in winter and open in summer. A voyage between Hamburg and
Yokohama is only 6,600 nautical miles via the northern sea route, a
40 per cent improvement over the traditional 11,400-nautical-mile
Suez route.

The Northwest Passage through Arctic Canada is of course
another such option, although some of its passages, even with
warming, can remain congested with thick ice. Last year, for the
first time in the era of satellite monitoring, both Arctic passages
were open for a brief amount of time during the same period. It is
expected that they will open for slightly longer periods each year in
the future thanks to global warming.

Huge oil and gas reserves and this potentially strategic shipping
channel have seen northern navies face off over land claims. The
Russians even went so far as to send a submarine to plant a national
flag under the North Pole to state their claims. Arctic sovereignty
anxiety will only increase in the coming years.

---

project and several other Chinese-funded and/or managed projects
were eventually moved to the Syrian capital of Damascus.

Does this sort of involvement risk China's traditionally official
neutral stance? What if the Chinese Harbour Construction Company
workers at the port had been bombed and killed? China may not
have been able to remain neutral, especially if strong domestic public
opinion was apparent, for example as that seen after incidents such

as the US bombing of the Chinese Embassy in Belgrade in 1999 or the Hainan Island spy plane incident in 2001, which both saw outpourings of Anti-American/Anti-Western sentiment across China. Beijing, as it moves outward to secure energy supplies and business, and protect the SLOCs, may well find itself compromised in terms of its traditional foreign policy.

CHAPTER FIVE

Piracy: The Nebulous Threat

Monday 6 October 2008 – The Riau Islands, Indonesia

Pirates come out of nowhere in the night, fast and quick in high-powered boats. They approach unseen when there is no moon to light the water, unheard when the wind is up. The charts of the Shinyo Ocean *are clearly marked, warning in block capitals:*

EXTREME RISK OF PIRACY – SET WATCHES – STEER CLEAR –
NO STOPPING.

In case the message is not clear enough, the cluster of small islands that make up the Riaus is circled in thick red maker pen. This is Asia's largest and most active concentration of pirates. After dinner the captain orders lockdown and we are confined aft in the blockhouse.

Two crewmen posted outside make do with a little food and flasks of tea, their standard-issue binoculars close to hand. Both are from India, which, along with the Philippines and Indonesia, has for decades crewed the world's commercial shipping. They are small men, smaller still when seen with the deck before them stretching out towards the prow to the length of more than three soccer pitches. They have no night-vision gear, no guns. The newly developed systems of collapsible electric fences that deliver a 9,000-volt shock at any point of contact (a painful but not deadly charge) and long-distance acoustic shockers cannot be used on oil tankers or other ships carrying heavily flammable materials. There is only one real option – the fire hoses. Simple, but effective.

The pirates of the Malacca Straits and the South China Sea are traditional and, unlike their peers off the Somali coast, have yet to acquire rocket-propelled grenades. They prefer handguns, or more usually just knives, machetes and cutlasses, with which it is easy enough to subdue the crew of a boarded vessel. The trick is to keep the pirates from boarding in the first place. Oil tankers carry powerful hoses. When set to 'fog' they are effective in dousing a shipboard fire; when set to 'straight stream' they blast a hard jet of salt water at up to 250 pounds per square inch, enough to capsize a small boat. When pirates appear, increasing speed is not necessarily a course of action open to the captain of a VLCC. Depending on water depth, cargo weight, tides and other factors to be calculated, going faster can take twenty to thirty minutes at the risk of creating suction that will bottom a boat in shallow waters.

The Riaus are comprised of the Riau, the Natuna, Anambas and Lingga Islands. A province of Indonesia, with Tajung Pinang as its capital, there can be no better place for pirates to hide – 3,200 islands among which a speedboat can quickly disappear. Shinyo Ocean's *watch reported that at 3.50 a.m. seven pirates armed with long knives boarded a nearby Panamanian-registered bulk carrier, the* JKM Muhieddine, *as it passed 64 nautical miles east of the Malaysian island Pulau Tioman. The vessel was steaming at 11 knots towards Singapore when the gang boarded her aft. Having subdued the carrier's master and another crewmember, they stole money and personal belongings – cameras, mobile phones, spare shoes and clothing – moving on to the chief engineer's cabin where they took his money, then tying up the captain. They made their getaway at 4.10 a.m.*

It was a busy night. The watch later learned that at 4.20 a.m., eight pirates in a speedboat, armed with long knives and metal pipes, had come alongside and boarded the chemical tanker Sun Geranium *in the same area as the* Muhieddine. *They took the bridge and tied up the two officers on duty before taking them to the master's cabin. The rest of the crew were tied up on the poop deck above the bridge aft. The pirates stole money, phones, cameras and valuables before speeding away.*

No one was injured in either attack; more worrying was the thought of two large ships under way at night in busy shipping lanes with no one at the wheel. Collision is a constant risk. The International Maritime Bureau's (IMB's) Piracy Reporting Centre in the Malaysian capital of Kuala Lumpur maintains a round-the-clock watch on acts of piracy and armed robbery in the Malacca and Singapore Straits and out across the South China Sea. By its reckoning, the same gang, well known in these waters, hit both ships.

'They're not pirates,' our captain said the next morning, 'they're just petty thieves.' Like any householder in a bad neighbourhood, there was little he could do but lock down the ship – even opening a door from inside the ship, just for a few minutes, requires a mountain of paperwork and places the ship's insurance at risk. Oil tankers now rarely get hit in the Malacca Straits or the South China Sea – the prospect of a 72-foot climb up a rope swinging from a grappling hook fired onto the deck sends pirates off in search of smaller carriers instead: mostly container ships – easier to sneak up on, board and flee. But around the Horn of Africa it's a different story.

Easy Money?

Who exactly the first pirate was is not known but it is safe to assume that he, or she (nautical history is littered with 'pirate queens'), ventured out to sea shortly after the first ship bearing a valuable cargo had left port with the express intention of robbing it. The term 'pirate' means simply 'one who plunders the sea' and the sea lanes of the globe have long been major transport routes for unimaginable wealth – commodities from sugar to silver, potential slaves, all manner of manufactured goods and, of course, oil.

Piracy, as the widely reported resurgence of activity off the Somali coast in recent years shows, flourishes where the rule of law is weakest. And while poverty, boredom and a perceived sense of injustice drive young men in cities to join street gangs, on the coasts adjacent to the world's SLOCs communities, impoverished by economic instability, ignored by governments and encouraged by corrupt and conniving officials, young men turn to piracy. In Somalia, the world's current pirate hotspot, for communities deprived of a livelihood by the incursion of factory ships from various nations as well as over-fishing (Somalians claim that in the region of US$300 mn of tuna, shrimp and lobster are being stolen every year by illegal trawlers) piracy (which is also often the resurrection of an old tradition) offers a route to seemingly easy money.

Political instability drives piracy – the unravelling of Indonesia's Suharto regime in the mid-1990s saw a surge in pirate activity around the Riau Islands, with the Straits of Malacca and Singapore as well as the South China Sea all becoming hotspots. Frequent bouts of political instability and virtual civil war in the southern Philippines have fuelled piracy in the Celebes Sea; internal conflicts have driven the pirates to sea in Somalia, Nigeria and half a dozen other African countries. Piracy thrives, indeed relies, on instability.

Box 5.1 The Rise of the Pirates: Areas Prone to Piracy

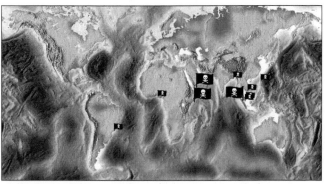

Fig. 5.1 Beware! Key areas of piracy globally

South Asia

Bangladesh: Although the number of attacks has fallen in recent years, the area is still considered high risk. Pirates are targeting ships preparing to anchor, with most reported attacks at the anchorages and approaches to Chittagong.

East Asia

Indonesia: in particular, the Anambas and Natuna island area (the Riaus), Belawan and Jakarta's Tandjung Priok harbour. Pirates are usually armed with knives and machetes, occasionally with guns. Many attacks in this area are believed to have gone unreported.

Malacca Straits: the number of reported attacks has dropped following intensive and aggressive patrols by the littoral states (primarily Singapore and Malaysia). Since 2005 all ships transiting through the 2.7-mile-wide Straits are maintaining strict anti-piracy watches. The patrols continue.

Malaysia: the waters off Tioman Island (20 miles east of the Malaysian peninsula) in the South China Sea remain prone to random piracy.

Singapore Straits: the IMB's Piracy Reporting Centre advises all vessels to continue to be vigilant and maintain anti-piracy watches around Singapore. Pirates are still attacking ships while under way or while anchored outside Singapore port limits.

Philippines: Manila – pirates are still targeting ships at anchor and in the surrounding waters. Additionally, frequent bouts of political instability in the southern Philippines continue to fuel piracy in the Celebes Sea with acts of piracy reported offshore from Mindanao's General Santos City. Some pirate activity has also been reported off the northern tip of Luzon and the Batan and Babuyan Islands.

Vietnam: piracy offshore the southern Vietnamese city of Vung Tau (which is also the crude oil extraction centre of Vietnam) continues.

Africa and Gulf of Aden

Ghana: a growing number of attacks have been reported while ships are anchored at Tema near Accra in south-east Ghana.

Nigeria: extremely violent pirates have attacked and robbed vessels as well as kidnapped crews along the coast and creeks around Lagos, Port Harcourt and along the Bonny River anchorages, ports and surrounding waters. Nigeria's entire coastline is considered to be at hazard from piracy, according to the IMB's Piracy Reporting Centre.

Tanzania: pirates continue to target ships at port, anchorages and surrounding waters close to Dar es Salaam.

Gulf of Aden: Somali pirates are regularly attacking vessels along the northern Somali coast in the Gulf of Aden. These pirates have displayed and used automatic weapons and rocket-propelled grenades (RPG) in attempts to board and hijack vessels. All vessels maintain strict twenty-four-hour visual and radar anti-piracy watches.

Somalia: Somali pirates have resumed attacking vessels off both the eastern and southern coasts of Somalia as far as the Kenyan and Tanzanian coasts. Somali pirates are armed with automatic weapons and RPGs and use 'mother ships' to launch attacks further away from the coast. 'Mother ships' are able to proceed further out to sea and then launch smaller boats to attack and hijack passing ships. Pirate attacks have occurred up to 500 nautical miles from the Somali coast. The IMB now advises vessels not making scheduled calls to Somali ports to keep as far away as possible from the Somali coast, preferably over 600 nautical miles.

South and Central America and the Caribbean
Brazil: in recent years the number of reported attacks has dropped in the Port of Santos area; attempted assaults on vessels are still occasionally reported.

Source: Authors' research and the IMB Piracy Reporting Centre

As prosperity rises and political stability holds, so piracy tends to recede. One would be hard pressed to find a pirate along the Fujian coast today (despite there being plenty of smugglers transporting everything from petrol to Mercedes Benz cars into China) but in the warlord-wracked China of the early twentieth century it was a notorious pirate haven. The Bugis pirates were swept out of Singapore long ago, Hong Kong is no longer the haven for pirate commanders that it was until the late 1930s, while even the once infamously notorious waters of the Caribbean are almost pirate free. India, China and Japan's navies are now part of the international policing effort protecting the sea lanes from pirates off the Somali coast. However, in Indonesia and the Philippines, where government authority remains uncertain and fragile, high-powered speedboats still come out of the night to threaten passing ships.

To date, there have appeared no clear and verifiable links between the pirates operating around the Horn of Africa and off the Somali coast with Islamist terrorist groups. However, links have been made between piracy and terrorism in other parts of the world, notably the Philippines. Authorities like to make a distinction between what can be termed 'non-political piracy' and 'maritime terrorism', despite the fact that it can often be difficult to separate the two. The former is good old-fashioned robbery and kidnapping for profit, and the latter committing acts of piracy on the high seas to promote a political, ideological or religious cause. To date, the Somali pirates have not identified themselves with a cause (though they may be paying 'taxes' to Islamist groups in the region to ensure their freedom to operate). However, in the Malacca Straits groups of pirates have identified themselves explicitly with the Free Aceh Movement (*Gerakan Aceh Merdeka* – GAM) and claim to have used ransoms from the kidnapping of ships ands crews to fund GAM. Similarly, in the Philippines both the Moro National Liberation Front (MNLF) and the Abu Sayyaf Group (ASG) have used piracy as a means to raise funds. However, examples of pure maritime terrorism against commercial ships of a specific country (as distinct from naval vessels and incidents such as the suicide bomb attack on the *USS Cole* in 2000 and other similar events) are rare and the potential tactic of hijacking a particular vessel to use as a floating bomb by sailing it into a port and exploding it so far unknown.

Whether a pirate's motivation is ideological or simply financial, commercial shipping must take precautions. When the authors of this book sailed through the Singapore Straits and past the Riau Islands in October 2008 on a VLCC, pirate watch was maintained from early evening until sunrise. Our ship was a giant of the seas – 1,100 feet long, 200 feet wide, riding 72 feet out of the ocean. The vessel itself was worth around US$130 mn and was carrying 180,000 tonnes of oil from Fujairah to Taiwan. The client was one of Taiwan's largest industrial concerns and the vessel made the trip, under charter to the Taiwanese, repeatedly – unloading on the island's heavily industrialised west coast before heading back to Fujairah, refilling and then returning again to Taiwan. The circuit of loading and unloading carries on without a break in order to keep the export-driven plastics industry of Taiwan operating.

Close to the Port of Singapore the Singapore Navy's sleek Formidable-class stealth frigates, the most advanced surface combat craft anywhere in South East Asia, are a common sight in the shipping lanes, darting from tanker to tanker, like a collie dog shepherding a flock of sheep. However, only a few hours out of Singapore, close to the Indonesian Riau Islands, there are no other vessels in sight. Despite having locked down the ship and stationed two crew members aft on pirate watch, our captain was relatively blasé about piracy, noting that no VLCC had ever been taken by pirates – they were too tricky to board, the powerful hoses would force the pirates to retreat and, anyway, what would some guys from a small Indonesian fishing village do with 180,000 tonnes of crude oil? We felt reassured.

A month later, at 10 a.m. on Saturday 15 November 2008, Somali pirates hijacked the recently launched *MV Sirius Star*, a brand new and gleaming VLCC, owned and operated by a subsidiary of the Saudi Arabian state oil company Saudi Aramco and registered under a Liberian flag of convenience. It was the largest ship ever captured by pirates. The ship was en route from Saudi Arabia to the United States via the Cape of Good Hope. At the time of the attack, it was about 450 nautical miles[1] south-east of the coast of Kenya, with a crew of twenty-five and its tanks fully loaded with Saudi oil. The ship itself was estimated to be worth approximately US$150 mn, and its cargo, equivalent to just over one-quarter of Saudi Arabia's daily oil production output, worth at least US$100 mn. Not only was this a new record in terms of the size of vessel hijacked but the *MV Sirius Star*'s distance from shore meant that the pirates must have journeyed for three or four days to reach her. The pirates anchored the hijacked tanker at the port of Harardhere in Mudug province, central Somalia, kept the twenty-five crew hostage and issued a US$25 mn ransom demanded via Al Jazeera television. The pirates later reduced their ransom demand to US$15 mn. The *MV Sirius Star* and all its crew were released on 9 January 2009 after a ransom of US$3 mn had been dropped onboard the ship from a helicopter. Five of the pirates (who apparently numbered 'dozens' in total) were reported drowned when their boat capsized in a storm after leaving the *MV Sirius Star*. The body of one washed ashore with US$153,000 in cash in a plastic bag.

The *MV Sirius Star* hijacking by Somali pirates showed all too clearly that, despite the unprecedented international effort in response to the sudden and alarming rise in piracy in the area, involving naval forces from NATO, the EU, China, Russia, India, Japan and others patrolling the Horn of Africa region, the pirates were still active, bold and not apparently that worried.

Bad Business on the High Seas

Piracy happens because it is lucrative. In 2008 ship owners paid pirates over US$40 mn for scores of ships (forty-two in 2008 alone) and hundreds of crewmembers.[2] This was just Somalia and just ransom demands – globally the IMB estimates that maritime piracy costs transport vessels between US$13–15 bn a year in losses when stolen cargo and goods, thefts of crew's belongings and ship equipment as well as delays in port while the attack is reported and investigated, not forgetting increased insurance rates, are factored in as well.[3] The recent resurgence of piracy has spawned an industry of ransom negotiators, lawyers, private security operatives and ransom delivery teams around the world, notably in the UK as London has historically been the centre of maritime dispute resolution. It is a complex and sophisticated business – on all sides. According to Euan Air, the general manager of Hart Supply Chain Security, a firm that deploys private armed guards onboard commercial shipping (a significant growth industry in 2009),[4] some ship owners are now installing onboard private security guards and razor wire barriers around the stern and lowest points of access to their vessels, even placing dummies along the ship's railings to give the illusion of additional lookouts. Ransom negotiators are using robot camera planes to verify that crew members are still alive, while pirates are using automatic identification systems to track ships and insider information to identify the vessels they are targeting. In South East Asia the main aim of the pirates is to steal goods and cargo. However, off the coast of Somalia and around the Horn of Africa ransom demands are moveable feasts tending to start extremely high but open to negotiation. Those involved in ransom negotiations report that the Somali pirates are well informed about ship movements, cargoes, owners and the presence of naval patrols.

Pirates of Somalia

Somalia is a classic example – a failed state since the government collapsed in 2001 and a subsequent bloody inter-clan conflict that neither outside intervention or any internal attempt at reconciliation has been able to solve. The collapse of Somalia's economy and a functioning state apparatus appears to be almost total and yet Somali GDP per capita has remained higher than in many neighbouring countries – business has survived, trade has continued and piracy plays a central part in that.

The majority of Somali pirate raids are launched from the Puntland region of north-eastern Somalia. Pirates operate out of a growing range of other African locations including Nigeria as well as up to the Republic of Djibouti and across the Gulf of Aden in the Republic of Yemen. Approximately one-third of Somalia's population lives in Puntland, which declared itself an autonomous state in 1998 but does not seek outright independence from the capital Mogadishu. Puntland is a poor province divided by clan rivalries despite rumours of oil off the coast; piracy has now become a central part of the region's fragile economy. The Puntland coast is ideal territory for pirates – 1,000 miles of largely unguarded and ineffectively patrolled coastline. Coastal dwellers claim to have been pushed into piracy because their traditional livelihood – fishing – has become untenable. Since the early 1990s factory ships from various nations equipped with heavy trawls and other unlawful fishing equipment have moved into Puntland's offshore waters, the traditional fishing grounds of the Puntland Somalis. These ships have consistently violated catch regulations, including keeping their catch alive and then stocking it in waters closer

Fig. 5.2 Somali pirates captured off the Horn of Africa

to their home bases, where fishing has been depleted. Essentially the waters off Puntland have been overfished, remain unstocked and the local fishermen are unable to make a living wage. The fishermen did attempt to fight back using speedboats to dissuade the trawlers, or at least levy a 'tax' on them, but the trawlers kept on coming. The independent Somalian news organisation *WardheerNews* found 70 per cent of Somalians 'strongly supported piracy as a form of national defence'.[5]

In desperation many of these coastal dwellers have now turned to crime and been recruited by the pirate gangs. As piracy attacks grew off the Somali coast, they initially appeared to reflect the economic grievances and frustrations of the local community: many 'hostage ships' were factory fishing ships from a variety of countries including Iran, China and Kenya, which directly threatened the livelihoods of the coastal villagers. However, things then escalated both in terms of targets and ransoms: larger and larger cargo ships began to be hijacked and larger and larger ransoms demanded, culminating in the audacious capture of the *MV Sirius Star*.

The Global Response to the Resurgence of Piracy in Africa: One Year of Activity

April 2008: the IMB's Piracy Reporting Centre calls for additional security measures off Somalia's northern coast following an attack on the French cruise ship *Le Ponant*. This is the first formal recognition that pirate activity off Somalia has moved up the country's coastline into the Gulf of Aden as a result of earlier measures taken by the international community to combat piracy off the country's long eastern coastline. The French military capture six Somali pirates involved in the hijacking of the *Le Ponant*. However the IMB maintains that Nigeria remains the leading global piracy hotspot. In the same week Somali pirates fire on a Japanese VLCC.

June 2008: the World Food Programme (WFP) states that it will be forced to stop shipments of humanitarian aid to Somalia within two weeks unless it can find a navy willing to escort the vessels it charters. Over 90 per cent of WFP food shipments to Somalia arrive by sea. Canada agrees to escort WFP-chartered vessels until September 2008.

July 2008: the situation with kidnapped ships escalates when the Japanese owners of the *Stella Maris* – a bulk carrier seized by Puntland-based pirates – receive a ransom demand for US$3 mn.

August 2008: armed pirates off the Somali coast hijack a Malaysian chemical tanker, the *Bunga Melati Dua*, carrying a cargo of palm oil from Indonesia to Rotterdam. A Filipino crew member is killed in the attack. Ten days later a second Malaysian vessel, sailing to Singapore from Saudi Arabia, is attacked. Somali pirates take the Japanese chemical tanker *Irene* hostage along with its twenty-five crew. As the list of kidnapped and attacked ships grows, so coalition naval forces in the Gulf of Aden establish a patrol zone to offer merchant vessels safe passage off the coast of Somalia.

September 2008: Somali pirates seize a French yacht with two passengers onboard. A day later an Egyptian cargo ship is captured and then a Hong Kong-flagged vessel, the *Stolt Valor*, a chemical tanker with a crew of twenty-two, bringing the number of vessels known to be in the hands of Somali pirates to ten. However, a German-owned vessel and its thirteen crew members are released after three weeks in captivity for a reportedly 'low seven-digit US dollar' ransom. Despite this the situation escalates towards the end of the month with the capture by Somali pirates of a Ukrainian ship, the *Faina*, carrying around thirty Soviet-era tanks, other weapons and spare parts for armoured vehicles. The Russian Navy dispatches warships to the region a day before the *Faina* is taken.

October 2008: the EU begins naval escorts across the Gulf of Aden using French Navy corvettes while Indian Navy frigates arrive in African waters. Despite this a Greek chemical tanker, the *Genius*, is ambushed, chased and fired upon by Somali pirates before being captured. The Japanese vessel *Irene* and its twenty-five crew are released after a US$1.6 mn ransom is paid. Pirates demand US$8 mn for the *Stolt Valor*, its cargo and crew. Further ships are attacked – NATO agrees to participate in anti-piracy operations off Somalia and to send seven frigates to the Gulf of Aden while the EU Naval Task Force agrees to protect WFP-chartered ships. However, the growing international effort looks shaky as Malaysia withdraws two of its warships from the Gulf of Aden, saying ship owners will have to invest in their own security.

November 2008: actions against the pirates escalate as coalition aircraft drop smoke bombs on pirate skiffs to thwart an attack on a tanker sailing through the Gulf of Aden and German helicopters repel pirates threatening a ship. British private security guards repel a Somali pirate attack on a chemical tanker. However, the same week pirates seize a Saudi VLCC, the Iranian bulk carrier *Delight*, carrying wheat, and a second oil tanker, the *Chemstar Venus*. The *Stolt Valor* is finally released following an undisclosed ransom payment. The global shipping community is shocked when pirates hijack the *MV Sirius Star* oil tanker, the largest ship ever captured by pirates. The UN toughens sanctions against Somalia in the light of the dramatic rise in attacks on commercial vessels.

December 2008: attacks on shipping, including a passenger cruise ship, continue as the UN Security Council extends its authorisation for nations to enter Somalian waters to pursue and attack pirates (provided they have the go-ahead from the Somalian government).

Air and naval operations involving EU member states commence off the Somali coast relieving NATO forces. Almost immediately the German frigate *Karlsruhe* foils a pirate attack on an Egyptian bulk carrier off the Yemeni coast. The Security Council also authorises countries fighting piracy to take action on Somalian territory and in Somalian airspace. Somali pirates attack a Chinese fishing boat, the *Tianyu No.8*, the first Chinese vessel targeted to date. Days later naval forces and the ship's crew repel a pirate attack on a Chinese-owned semisubmersible heavylift ship.[6] Beijing responds by deploying People's Liberation Navy vessels to escort Chinese shipping in the Gulf of Aden.

January 2009: the EU implements a new 'get tough' policy and foils pirate attacks on six vessels; French naval forces capture nineteen Somali pirates and the US unveils plans for a dedicated anti-piracy naval force to patrol the Gulf of Aden. The Japanese government announces that it will submit a bill to parliament, the Diet, by March that, if approved, will allow the country's armed forces to join anti-piracy operations. Somali pirates free the Turkish cargo ship, *Yasa Neslihan,* the Iranian *Delight* and the *MV Sirius Star* after undisclosed ransoms are paid. The coalition effort increases with twenty-four countries and five major international organisations cooperating at the UN to form the Contact Group on Piracy off the Coast of Somalia charged with coordinating anti-piracy actions in the Gulf of Aden. Italy contributes a frigate and South Korea dispatches its first destroyer to join anti-piracy forces. Despite this pirates capture a German-owned LPG tanker participating in a naval convoy through the Gulf of Aden Maritime Security Patrol Area, after the pirates have successfully diverted Chinese and Indian warships with a decoy raid.

February 2009: the EU-funded Maritime Security Centre – Horn of Africa (MSCHOA) is created. The *Faina*, with thirty tanks and other weaponry aboard, is released after US$3.2 mn in cash is air-dropped onto the ship by helicopter, making this the highest ransom payment in the region to date. China's *Tianyu No.8* and twenty-four crew captured in December are released. Singapore joins the international anti-piracy patrols with ships and helicopters. The Contact Group on Piracy claims it is reducing the level of incidents. On the same day another large cargo vessel is hijacked despite sailing within the designated Maritime Security Patrol Area under naval protection.

March 2009: attacks continue despite the stepped up coalition naval presence, with two attacks on vessels in two days involving the use of RPGs while a Chinese bulk carrier is strafed with machine-gun fire. Following an amendment to the country's traditionally pacifist constitution, the Japanese Diet is able to send two destroyers and some patrol aircraft to the Gulf of Aden. However, days later pirates seize two bulk carriers and then attack a further three vessels.

April 2009: Somali pirate attacks continue while a rise in attacks by Nigerian pirates spreads out coalition naval and air forces on both the east and west coasts of Africa. Pirates off the north-eastern coast of Somalia capture a French yacht with four crew members. US Navy marines shoot dead three Somali pirates and free a hostage during an attempted seizure of the *Maersk Alabama* container ship. Meanwhile French forces capture a pirate 'mother ship' used as a base for raids further out to sea. The *Stolt Valor* and her twenty-two crew are freed after over six months.

Since April 2009 attacks on ships in the Gulf of Aden, around the Horn of Africa and on the eastern coast of Africa near Nigeria have continued. For its part the two-dozen-nation naval coalition has continued to try to protect the Gulf of Aden Maritime Security Patrol Area and the escorted and protected shipping lanes. Efforts, led by the French Navy have also continued to put the pirate's 'mother ships' out of action, while the British Royal Navy has started boarding and searching smaller skiffs closer to shore.

However, looking at the events that took place between April 2008 and April 2009, we get a sense of how serious and widespread the new threat of Somali and Gulf of Aden piracy is – multiple ship hijackings up to VLCC class, significant ransom payments, crew killed, bazookas, RPGs and automatic weapons regularly fired. We also get a sense of what a mammoth international effort has been made to try to keep the SLOCs around the Horn of Africa, the Gulf of Aden and the Somali coastline secure for uninterrupted shipping. This has been a massive effort in terms of time and money, manpower and materials as well as a great deal of diplomacy in places from the UN Security Council to the Japanese parliament.

Despite this, by September 2009, security research company Risk Intelligence was predicting that there would be over 300 attacks in the Gulf of Aden before the end of the year compared with 141 attacks in 2008.[7] It is also worth remembering that while the overwhelming focus has been on Somalia, piracy has not gone away elsewhere. In October and November 2008, while NATO was deploying frigates to the Gulf of Aden, at least four vessels were attacked by pirates close to the narrow sea passage of Batu Berhanti in the Singapore Straits. In its report for 2008 the IMB noted that in Asia there had been an increase in the number of actual piracy incidents in 2008 compared to 2007.[8] Our captain on the *Shinyo Ocean* is neither so blasé nor sleeping so soundly now.

The East Asian Energy Angle

Attacks on vessels transporting energy-related products including oil now represent a significant percentage of overall maritime piracy attacks – a resurgent percentage in recent years that is likely to grow further now VLCCs are being hijacked and oil tankers form the majority of energy-carrying vessels are being targeted. This is up from just 12 per cent of total attacks in 2006 to over 24 per cent in 2007 and rising.[9] While these attacks do not usually involve the theft of the energy cargo itself they can delay, hinder and sometimes halt the shipment of thousands of tonnes of oil, with the threat of interrupted supplies to the consumer nation. And in some extreme cases the energy is actually lost – in April 1998 Indonesian pirates seized the *MV Petro Ranger* (owned by a Singaporean national but flying the Malaysian flag) carrying 9,600 tons of diesel petroleum and 1,200 tons of A-1 jet fuel outside Singaporean waters en route to Vietnam. The vessel was sailed to the Chinese island of Hainan where it was repainted, renamed the *MV Wilby* and reflagged as a 'phantom vessel' while other pirate ships siphoned off half of the estimated US$2.3 mn cargo.[10] The Chinese authorities arrested the pirates and charged them with smuggling though they only received a few months in jail.

Table 5.1 **Pirate attacks on energy vessels: a new wave**

Year	Attacks on energy vessels (as a % of total acts of piracy)
2001	17
2002	16
2003	15
2004	16
2005	14
2006	12
2007	24
2008	22
2009*	27

Source: IMB Piracy Reporting Centre
Note: * = as of end first half of 2009

A high percentage of these attacks on energy-carrying vessels have occurred while the ships have been en route to East Asia. Aside from the potential for interruption to their essential oil supplies this gives rise to several concerns for the consuming and oil import dependent nations of East Asia. First, the most significant rise in attacks on energy vessels has been in and around Nigerian waters. China and other East Asian nations are sourcing increasing amounts of oil here, investing in Nigeria's oil industry and making it increasingly likely their shipments will be targeted. Second, there is the possibility that an oil tanker could be hijacked and used as a terrorist weapon.

The result of the upsurge in piracy and specifically attacks on energy-carrying vessels has seen an unprecedented involvement in the international anti-piracy effort by China and the other nations of East Asia. However, this has not been without problems for those governments; problems that may be exacerbated in the future. In China the initial deployment of naval vessels was, of course, not subject to approval by anyone but senior leaders and military personnel or deemed suitable as a subject for public discussion in the media, but does represent a break with the country's traditional reticence to become involved in either long-range ('blue water') or multilateral naval efforts. In South Korea the deployment of military vessels involved a motion to the National Assembly (the country's parliament) in Seoul that was hotly debated in February 2009.

In Japan the decision to despatch naval vessels to African waters was also the subject of intense debate given the country's post-war pacifist constitution. The special bill concerning anti-piracy missions submitted to the Japanese parliament (the Diet) by the government in early March 2009 (and passed the following June) included a stipulation that would allow Japan's Maritime Self-Defense Force (MSDF) personnel to fire directly at pirate vessels to stop acts of piracy and to construct base facilities in Djibouti (America's only military base on the African continent) – the first time the MSDF has been allowed to use weapons beyond the current limit of self-defence or emergency evacuation during overseas missions. This was controversial and the bill was passed only after a second vote in the Lower House, having been voted down by the Upper House as well as causing a breakdown over the issue between the ruling parliamentary bloc (led by the ruling Liberal Democratic Party) and the main opposition party (the Democratic Party of Japan). Traditionally, Japan has contributed financially to anti-piracy efforts and still does – for instance, in 2009 Tokyo gave significant amounts of aid to Malaysia's customs and police departments to boost Malaysia's maritime security efforts in the Malacca Straits. However, the controversial anti-piracy bill has ramifications for Japan's post-war approach to military action far beyond patrolling the seas around the Horn of Africa.

Looking to the future, a second contentious issue is whether or not the example of the combining together by various national navies can be extended to other parts of the world to better guarantee the security of the SLOCs and perhaps also see navies increasingly cooperate to ensure security in various trouble spots. Wu Shengli, the Commander Admiral of China's navy, told the Chinese state news agency *Xinhua* in April 2009 that, 'It is the obligation of the naval forces of all countries to work together to ensure the safety of the oceans ... exchanges and co-operation between naval forces of different countries will enhance mutual trust and development.'[11] But this is not always what is happening as East Asia's navies, and those of the wider Pacific Rim, extend their traditional remits. The Indian Ocean, the Pacific, the Taiwan Straits and the South China Sea are all examples of places where new problems are arising.

The rise of the Chinese Navy and its increasing commitments raises issues across the Pacific, which has traditionally been seen as largely American controlled in conjunction with partner nations such as Japan and South Korea. Additionally the long-standing relationship between Taiwan and the US has frequently raised the role of both the Chinese and US navies in the Taiwan Straits. Some strategic analysts have gone so far as to suggest that the Pacific should be formally divided into spheres of control – the eastern Pacific under Chinese control and the western under US control. This is improbable in the short to medium term, though veteran China watchers, such as David Shambaugh, believe that there will be a more shared role in policing the Pacific and that the US should be open to China, Japan and the US jointly working together on the security of the East Asia's SLOCs to everyone's benefit.[12] What is certain is that in terms of its security the Pacific is no longer effectively an 'American lake'.

But it is perhaps the Indian Ocean and the proximity of Indian and Chinese naval vessels where relations have become most fraught with potentially far-reaching geopolitical consequences. New Delhi has had at least one ship in the Gulf of Aden since October 2008, and shortly afterwards China deployed two warships to the same area – all on anti-piracy patrol and aiming to prevent any hindrance to their respective countries' supplies of oil and commercial shipping. However, both countries have eyed each other warily due in part to mutual distrust dating back to the Sino-Indian War of 1962 and China's traditional backing of Pakistan (which is much less obvious now in a period dominated by the prerequisites of trade and investment), and in part to China's construction of naval stations and refuelling ports in Burma, Sri Lanka, Bangladesh and Pakistan. What has been described as China's 'string of pearls' – ports, staging posts and hubs – some analysts in India view as apparent encirclement and this is creating political tensions between New Delhi and Beijing and fuelling the ire of highly vocal nationalists in both countries. In the future the issue of the Indian Ocean and Sino-Indian relations in that region will become far more important.

Where Do We Go from Here?

Some major questions arise from the ongoing efforts against piracy in the Malacca Straits, the South China Sea, the Indian Ocean and particularly around the Horn of Africa. A primary concern is whether or not the current multinational combined navy patrols can reduce the threat of piracy in those regions? There is some evidence that increased patrols have achieved this in the Malacca Straits and through the Singapore Straits to the Riaus and into the South China Sea. However, Graeme Gibbon Brooks, the managing director of Dryad Maritime Intelligence Services, a British company that provides intelligence to mariners worldwide, has commented that, 'there will never be enough warships' to secure all of the Indian Ocean by patrol.[13] While incidences of piracy remain in those regions (largely affecting container ships rather than oil tankers) the number has been reduced from its height in the 1980s. The issue of piracy around the Horn of Africa is a somewhat different question given the enhanced capabilities and daring of the pirates in those waters, their firepower and large ransom demands, the expanse of sea involved, their apparent immunity from serious prosecution in Somalia, and the far larger patrols occurring as ever more countries participate. Piracy in that region is expected to get worse before it gets better as the pirates become apparently more organised and experienced in dealing with the international coalition. This is already being seen in the extensive use of 'mother ships' to extend the range of piracy acts out to sea and night-time raids complete with US-Army-issue night-vision goggles.

All this is placing extreme burdens on ship owners. It is clear that Somali pirates are continuing to squeeze ransoms out of the owners as they become savvier negotiators. It is apparent that there is little internal discussion within the industry about ransom amounts. Victim companies remain in the dark about the going rates, increasingly using third-party agents (with the ability to manipulate negotiations, according to some sceptical observers) who act on behalf both of the owners and the pirate gangs. The cost of ransom insurance is now prohibitively high (in 2008 alone 'K&R', or kidnap and ransom insurance rates, rose from an average of US$500 for a voyage across the Gulf of Aden to in excess of US$20,000[14]) and a growing number of ship owners are hiring and deploying armed private security guards on tankers. (Some, including Britain's Royal Navy, have advised owners that the presence of these guards may only lead to an escalation of violence during attacks and the greater threat of crew deaths.) Other ship owners have decided to swallow the additional cost of rerouting ships to avoid the pirates, bypassing the Suez Canal and travelling via the Cape of Good Hope, which as well as requiring additional time and bunker fuel also effectively puts shipping back almost a century and a half. The canal was opened in 1869 precisely to allow water transportation between Europe and Asia without the need to navigate around Africa.

For the moment, ship owners will mostly continue to pay ransoms in order to recover their ships and safeguard the lives of their crews (no small matter – the IMO calculates that since 1995, over 350 sailors have died in pirate attacks worldwide – roughly thirty sailors a year[15]) until a solution is found at an international level. Despite complaints about ransom payments from some countries, notably Spain, ransom payments will continue to be paid as long as there are no proven links between piracy and terrorism. Were such links to exist, it would then become a distinctly different issue involving governments, and for owners to negotiate and pay ransoms would become illegal.

Eventually these substantial additional costs are passed along to shipping customers. For ship owners the problem lies with the inability of the naval forces and world governments to resolve the situation – Somali pirates are invariably arrested, returned to Somalia and soon released to become pirates again. Many in the shipping community ask a very simple question – if these were aeroplanes and not commercial ships being hijacked and ransomed, surely the governments and security forces of the world would take distinctly more interest? It's a fair question and once again reflects the media and the public's general lack of knowledge regarding the importance of transportation by sea.

There is also the fear that newly resurgent incidents of piracy in Asia, particularly along the Malacca Straits and around the Singapore Straits, may in part be influenced by the Somali experience (not that there are currently any formal links between African and Asian pirates). In view of ship owners paying million-dollar ransoms and apparently willing to drop large bags of cash on to the decks of hijacked ships, pirates in these areas may seek to emulate their Somali counterparts.

If the continuing patrols fail to reduce the incidence of piracy sufficiently then some may feel the need to extend the current protection to another level: to develop a strategy actively to suppress the pirates of the region. The long history of piracy is littered with the attempts of various governments and their navies to launch suppression and eradication campaigns – invariably they were extremely bloody and never fully effective. Many of the routes in South East Asia where piracy still exists were the preserve of the British East India Company in the seventeenth and eighteenth centuries. Piracy was such a plague that the Admiralty in London granted the company permission to punish pirates. Those captured were hanged from the yardarm, or flogged, their foreheads branded with the letter P. In the early 1800s Singapore merchants petitioned the Royal Navy and a bounty was set on the head of each pirate killed or captured. Royal Navy captains, always with an eye to boosting their wages, vigorously pursued their new prey and the purse that went with it. Suppressions repeatedly occurred but eradication was never total. As the pirates in African waters today are not dissimilar from the pirates of the seventeenth and eighteenth centuries in Asia – loose agglomerations of people affiliated largely to no nation or political cause – they are able simply to melt into their communities, disappear and then reappear when the suppression efforts subside. That is the nebulousness of the threat of piracy.

CHAPTER SIX

The Criminalisation of Crews

28 May 2008 – Taean County, Republic of Korea

Kim Chul-hwan points to the lapping waves ahead of him. Wistfully, he recalls his heyday bobbing out at sea three years ago. 'There wasn't really any need for skill,' he says. 'We literally just ladled the fish in. It was rich pickings for everyone. We'd just haul them in by the ton.'

The wrinkles on his worn face ease as he becomes animated about the different sea life that was once his regular catch, the wind blowing onshore and ruffling his hair. 'Groupers, sea bass, shrimps and conger eels were what we focused on most, while many of my family would make sure we'd get a big harvest of seaweed which sells well here. My cousin just focuses on crabs. In winter, there'd be oysters the size of this,' he says, folding his fingers into a fist. He kicks at the sand, his eyes glassy as he reminisces. 'And then one day the Yellow Sea here turned black,' Kim says quietly. 'Our lives weren't the same after that.'

Kim, sixty-one, has been a fisherman since he was eighteen. As he lived in Taean County on the west coast of South Korea his day job took him to some of the most densely populated aquatic areas in East Asia, a coastal region feted throughout the nation for its natural beauty. A hundred and twenty islands lie offshore of what was a pristine set of sandy beaches. The region became a national park in 1978 and was inundated by tourists for its rugged, spectacular views. Bird watchers flocked to see the annual migration of Baikal teals from Siberia. Photographers trained their lenses on the stunning sunsets, reputed to be the finest on the peninsula. Many local seafood festivals celebrated the abundance of the deep blue sea.

All this changed one stormy night in December 2007. Waves lashed as gusts of wind up to 50 miles an hour barrelled into shore. Most of the crew aboard the 269,605 dwt supertanker Hebei Spirit *were sleeping fitfully through the raging weather, the ship so large that only the very tallest waves made any impact on the black hull. The ship had moved to this anchorage 4 miles from shore, as per local port authority instructions, to avoid the worst ravages of the storm.*

Over at Daesan Port, however, the constant tugging and chafing of the cable that tied together a tugboat and a barge carrying a huge floating crane owned by shipbuilder Samsung Heavy Industries eventually snapped. The barge drifted from the port out to sea, into the vicinity of the single-hulled tanker, a dying breed of ship. Regulations have been set in place since the 1990s to phase out all single-hull tankers by 2010. New ships coming out of the yards have a double skin, making environmental disasters less likely. The crew onboard the Chinese-owned Hebei Spirit *were roused from their slumber and warned that an errant little barge, one-tenth the length of the tanker, had broken from its moorings.*

However, tankers of this scale do not simply switch on, start engines and sail off in seconds. A VLCC such as the Hebei Spirit *carrying 260,000 tonnes of oil, equivalent to 1.8 mn barrels, will typically take at least two hours before she is ready to move.*

The waves lashed, and despite the Yellow Sea being some 600 miles by 435 miles in surface area, as if drawn by a magnet the barge carrying its pincer-like crane drew inexorably closer to the supertanker. About an hour after authorities had first warned the captain of the Hebei Spirit *about the errant tug, the crew on board the tanker heard the unmistakeable screech and cavernous bang of metal hitting metal as the barge careened into the ship. It was 7 a.m. on 7 December 2007. Its cargo – the sharp crane – neatly punctured three holes in the side of the Chinese tanker's hull.*

Oil began to flow. It would continue to do so for days and was to become the worst oil spill in South Korean history, 10,800 tonnes gushing from the tanks like an industrial waterfall. Within two days of the spill, the oil slick was 21 miles long. The spill was about one-third of the size of that of the Exxon Valdez *which caused huge damage to the pristine coastline of Alaska back in 1989. The beaches and shoreside that had been the livelihood of Kim Chul-hwan and hundreds of other fishermen went from paradise to a black-stained vision of hell in the space of a morning.*

Twenty-four hours later hundreds of volunteers had flocked to Mallipo beach to help in the clean up. The media flashed images of oily birds and seas to a saddened, indignant Korean nation. Volunteer numbers spiralled in their thousands forming long, messy human chains, the public announcement system usually used by the beach lifeguards becoming central command. Then President Roh Moo-hyun declared Taean County and five surrounding counties disaster zones. Police, firefighters and soldiers were mobilised to battle the oil spill. A local hospital worked out of a fleet of ambulances to treat those with headaches and nausea caused by the oil stench. The thick, viscous oil spread everywhere, into every crevice; black slippery shoeprints tracked around nearby supermarkets as supplies were bought in to feed the clean-up crews working round the clock.

An American English teacher volunteering at Mallipo Beach said that on her first evening at the disaster site she could not see the beach. 'Not even in the moonlight,' she said. 'It was all blackness.' The nation was in shock. Cleanliness is a virtue on this peninsula. Constantly blaring images of such disturbing, polluting devastation saddened and enraged the population. Within a month, authorities were reporting that more than a million citizens had turned up at the site to help clean-up operations. The government promised retribution.

Korean Sojourn

The ensuing eighteen months would show that South Korean justice could be subverted in the name of politics and industry. The two senior officers of the *Hebei Spirit* would find themselves up against a tribal, partisan judiciary and an opponent, Samsung, who was the industrial pride of South Korea, a conglomerate at the forefront of the country's seemingly inexorable rise up the world GDP rankings.

Thirteen days after the spill, on 20 December, the Korean Coast Guard completed an initial investigation. According to their conclusions, blame was shared between the tug captains, the barge captain and the

Indian officers of the *Hebei Spirit*: Captain Jasprit Chawla and Chief Officer Syam Chetan. The tug captains and the barge captain were charged with negligence and violating South Korea's Marine Pollution Prevention Act. The officers of the *Hebei Spirit* were charged with violating marine law. Interrogation of the 'Hebei Spirit Two' – as they would later become known in the media – began in earnest, the oil spill still front-page national news.

Captain Chawla would later reflect that there were many times he did not think he would make it. On the first day of custody, Chawla was alone, his chief officer in a separate cell. Chawla's cell was so small his hands could touch either wall when he stretched out. The temperatures inside were sub-zero. Amenities were basic. He had the same pit to wash his hands, brush his teeth and use as a toilet. His cell lacked basic amenities such as soap. He was prevented from using a telephone. Interrogations could last up to twenty hours a day, with Chawla unable to tell whether his court-appointed translator was telling his side of the story verbatim.

Samsung blamed the tanker owner for the incident. The Chinese owner, Qinhuangdao-based Hebei Ocean Shipping Company (known as HOSCO Group), denied responsibility. The trial concluded on 24 June 2008, over six months later. The *Hebei Spirit* officers were exonerated, as were the personnel on the barge. The two tug captains were found guilty. Barge owners Samsung Heavy Industries were also fined. Samsung filed a petition. Despite their exoneration, the *Hebei Spirit*'s captain and chief officer continued to be detained in South Korea until December 2008, when they were sentenced to jail terms.

In previous cases of crew criminalisation around the world there had been little conjoint action. The *Hebei Spirit* incident piqued the imagination of industry bodies from Europe and Asia as well as the general public in the men's home country of India. A torrent of public statements flowed. Diplomatic channels from Beijing and New Delhi were used to try to persuade Seoul to relent on this clear perversion of justice.

On 7 July 2008 the International Transport Workers' Federation (ITF), which represents transport workers around the world and was the central campaigner for Chawla and Chetan, appealed to the South Korean authorities to allow the two *Hebei Spirit* officers found innocent

Fig. 6.1 An Indian officer at work on a VLCC

of causing the oil spillage to return home. The men, each with families back in India, gave assurances that they would return to South Korea as and when any further trial took place, following the local prosecutors' decision to appeal against the judgment that exonerated them of involvement in the spill. This demand was denied. Three weeks later, the world's leading shipping organisations, representing more than 90 per cent of the world merchant fleet, issued a joint statement to the president of Korea describing the decision to detain the ship's officers as 'unjustified, unreasonable and in contravention of the men's rights' and reminding the authorities that the trial had determined that another vessel was wholly responsible for the incident.

The growing worldwide dissenting chorus at the continued detention of these two seafarers was unparalleled by any seafarer's rights issue ever before. It became shipping's *cause célèbre*, alongside the growing green agenda.

Though owned by a Chinese concern, the *Hebei Spirit* was managed by a third-party company, a common occurrence in shipping, where technical matters are often handed to outside experts allowing the ship-owning company to focus solely on trading matters. The third-party ship manager in question was Monaco-headquartered V. Ships, the largest company of its kind in the world, providing services to more than 1,000 vessels. From the outset, the company, led by President and CEO Roberto Giorgi, had been vocal and outspoken in its defence of its employees. Later that summer Giorgi flew to South Korea. His findings were grim. He told the press of his concerns at recent developments, 'which point to collusion' between the South Korean authorities, prosecutors and Samsung Heavy Industries, and that the efforts of Samsung and prosecutors 'look to be designed to ensure that the master and chief officer are found guilty on appeal'. Giorgi added, 'I am worried that the captain and chief officer may not get a fair trial this time around.'[1]

Sure enough, December came around – the first anniversary of the spill with plenty of *vox populi* from Taean residents saying how their lives remained shattered – and the retrial went as predicted. Chawla and Chetan were convicted and imprisoned. For those outside Korea who had been following the protracted case, there was widespread revulsion at what clearly looked like scapegoating: a politically inspired decision, first, to assuage South Korean public opinion – the men were paraded outside the court in handcuffs – and, second, to ease the exposure of the owner of the barge, the mighty local hero Samsung.

There followed international condemnation as the two men were led away to serve their sentences. Both appealed. Chawla, found guilty of criminal negligence, was given an eighteen-month sentence, while his chief officer was given eight months. The two were also fined 20 mn Korean Won (US$14,000) and 10 mn Korean Won (US$7,000) respectively. The interminable case was set to drag on, the men now having been separated from their families in India for more than a year. ITF Maritime Coordinator Stephen Cotton commented: 'This is not justice. It's not even something close. What we have seen today is scapegoating, criminalisation and a refusal to consider the wider body of evidence that calls into question the propriety of the court. This decision is incomprehensibly vindictive and will impact on all professional mariners.'[2]

Rallies were planned around the world, South Korean products were boycotted by Indians, and international shipping bodies ratcheted up their rhetoric against the Seoul authorities. For instance, InterManager, the association for third-party ship managers, companies like V. Ships, complained to the UN Human Rights Commission over allegations that the two jailed officers were being badly treated in their South Korean jail. 'Captain Chawla and First Officer Chetan have been victimised for performing their jobs professionally and have been unfairly incarcerated for something they were not responsible for,' said Guy Morel, InterManager's General Secretary.[3]

The international campaign paid off in January 2009 as South Korea's Supreme Court released the two men on bail. They were then kept under house detention, still not able to fly home as they awaited another trial set for June 2009. Finally, on 11 June South Korea's High Court found both men not guilty of destruction of the tanker *Hebei Spirit*. The lesser charge of not doing enough to prevent an oil leak was not overturned, however, and the fines remained in place.

Commenting on the pair's retrial, ITF General Secretary David Cockroft said: 'We find it unacceptable that the lesser charge against them was never removed … We cannot however excuse the unfair criminalisation that they have undergone and the contradictory nature of the dual verdicts.'[4]

After more than 550 days being held on South Korean soil, the two men made their way home. It was an unprecedented case in terms of the worldwide attention it received, Chawla telling industry journal *Lloyd's List* that he and Chetan 'could never dream' their case would attract so much global attention. Sadly, it was also just one of many such instances.[5] Many others are locked up without a reporter, trade union or industry body in sight. V. Ships' Roberto Giorgi would later muse at a conference in Singapore that if his two employees had worked for a small owner or manager they could have ended up spending ten years in a South Korean jail.

Taiwan Trauma

Less than an hour into their flight back home to a large, colourful, raucous welcome reception on Indian soil, Chawla and Chetan would have passed over the island of Taiwan. Thirty-five thousand feet below another remarkable act of seafarer criminalisation was still playing out. This case also involved a VLCC, this time called *Tosa*,

Fig. 6.2 The *Hebei Spirit* spewing oil off the coast of Korea (top) and leaving a slick across the ocean (bottom)

owned and managed by one of Japan's major shipping companies, Nippon Yusen Kaisha (NYK).

The crew of the *Tosa* stand accused of colliding with a Taiwanese fishing trawler, killing two fishermen. Remarkably, the incident took place in April 2009 and the crew were held for three months without being charged – an illegal act that Taiwanese authorities refuse to explain or apologise about. The plight of the crew – held in illegal limbo – only really surfaced after the Hong Kong Shipowners Association (HKSOA) demanded to know what was going on, some media picked up on the story, and Taiwanese prosecutors in the county of Hualien on Taiwan's mountainous eastern coast were forced into action in July indicting the Indian captain, his Bangladeshi second officer and a Filipino seaman, on charges of 'involuntary manslaughter'.

There are more holes in this particular case than there were in the hull of the *Hebei Spirit*. In a statement to the press, the HKSOA said that it was 'once again, appalled and extremely disappointed at the continuing trend of so-called "developed" economies to treat seafarers with little regard for their basic human rights'.[6]

HKSOA's managing director, Arthur Bowring, commented:

Enough is enough. Quite apart from the questionable legalities involved in this instance, there are just too many seafarers being treated badly and without respect. Politicians must realise that we have had enough, and are not now prepared to sit quietly when seafarers are not afforded the basic human right of being presumed innocent unless proven guilty. Continuing to keep seafarers detained in such circumstances not only shows a total lack of regard for human rights but also, once again, the triumph of politics and public appeasement over the law. Treating seafarers with no respect for their dignity and professionalism not only reflects badly on the country concerned, but also greatly harms the industry's urgent recruitment efforts.[7]

Just as in South Korea, there are clear signs that scapegoats were found to appease a furious local population. The Panamanian flagged *Tosa* was on a voyage from South Korea to Singapore when a Taiwanese fishing boat, the *Shingtong Cheng #86*, was reported capsized, resulting in the tragic deaths of two fishermen. Despite clear evidence showing that the tanker was at least one hour from the position of the capsize, and despite no evidence of collision on the hull of the VLCC, the ship was taken from the high seas under Coast Guard escort into Taiwanese port waters and the watchkeepers, the second officer and an able seaman, as well as the ship's master, Captain Glen Patrick Aroza, were taken ashore into detention.

After the media attention, both the second officer and the able seaman were released from jail but not allowed to leave Taiwan as they awaited trial, while the ship's master remained behind bars. The master remained the only man in jail and yet he was asleep during the incident. He had instructed the crew to wake him if an accident occurred. No one had.

What Taiwanese prosecutors perhaps had not prepared for were the eloquent, single-minded investigations and deliberations carried out by the wife of Captain Azora, Preetha. She has waged a strong campaign to ridicule the charges against her husband and his crew members. She has suggested that the detention of the crew was against the United Nations Convention on the Law of the Sea (UNCLOS), and that the *Tosa* was 'diverted by force' from international waters. Speaking to the Indian press she quoted Article 97 of UNCLOS, saying, 'No arrest or detention of the ship, even as a measure of investigation, shall be ordered by any authorities other than those of the flag state,' which in *Tosa*'s case was Panama and not Taiwan. Mrs Aroza then delivered the bombshell that inspections of the hulls of the trawler and the *Tosa* revealed that there had been no physical contact between them.

Taiwanese prosecutors backtracked and claimed that the trawler had capsized due to the wake of the huge *Tosa* – this despite ship data that shows the tanker was 6 miles away from the trawler at the time of the capsizing incident. 'Any one with even a nodding acquaintance with ships and seas knows that it is impossible for a trawler of that size to capsize simply by the wake or waves created by a ship in calm seas [*wind force was 5/6 on the Beaufort Scale*] unless the trawler was inherently unstable and not seaworthy,' Mrs Aroza shot back, before concluding with a plea for a similar global outcry to that which followed the case of the *Hebei Spirit* Two. 'It would be naive to expect Taiwanese authorities to abide by international law unless sufficient pressure is brought upon them,' she said. 'Only media and political pressure can help now.'[8]

The Indian Seafarers' Federation went to New Delhi to urge the government to take action. Among the delegation were none other than Jasprit Chawla and Syam Chetan, who had been at home for only a month by then. The case continues. Sadly, this is not the first time Indian seafarers have been mistakenly snared by Taiwanese authorities. In 1996 Captain Raj Goel was detained for three and a half years in violation of international law before being proved innocent.

The cases of engineering judicial results to appease an angry local electorate are far too common and made easier when it comes to maritime-related cases as there are no international rules in place to govern every aspect of a seafarer's rights. Placating the irate, such as fisherman Kim Chul-hwan in Taean in the fierce eye of the local media, takes a greater priority than pursuing justice it seems. The rise of violent piracy, combined with images of seafarers wrongly accused and behind bars are not helping to fill the industry's critical shortage of officers and young people entering the crewing business. Crews – out at sea, out of mind – are vital for world trade to continue smoothly.

C.P. Wake, chief executive of the Nautical Institute, the international professional body for qualified seafarers, wrote following the December 2008 guilty verdict of the *Hebei Spirit* Two:

> When the two men were led from court in handcuffs, as common criminals, it was a tragedy on a personal level for proud, family men being made to suffer humiliation. It is also a tragedy for shipping. As an industry we face major problems in recruiting the young, talented people we need into the future. In attacking seafarers, in vilifying them and making them out to be criminals regardless of their actions, then we are in danger of effectively killing seafaring as a career, and in the process damaging world trade.[9]

He went on to list other areas around the world where the rights of seafarers were in trouble, citing many major tanker disasters of the past decade:

> It is worth remembering the proposed European Union regulations seeking to criminalise those involved in maritime accidents; the trial of Captain Mangouros of the *Prestige* and others, approaches in

Spain; Captain Laptalo of the *Coral Sea* and his colleagues have been deported from Greece despite eventually being found innocent in the 'drugs in bananas' case; France set out to criminalise all and sundry involved with the *Erika*; the *Tasman Spirit* eight had a torrid time in Pakistan; and Venezuela held the master of the *Nissos Amorgos* for many months; and these are only a high-profile selection of cases. There are many more instances.

He concluded:

> The time has come to understand and recognise the importance of professional seafarers, not to view them as scapegoats to be threatened and made to suffer at the hands of unenlightened politicians and judiciary. Enough is enough, and the pall of criminalisation, which hangs so heavy on the profession, needs to be lifted immediately.[10]

Sadly his words have fallen on deaf ears.

Box 6.1   Shipping's Bill of Rights

There are more than 1.2 mn seafarers in the world's international merchant fleet and yet for decades there has been no uniform protection for this vital workforce, thanks in no small part to ship owners' desire to flag outside their own country with nations who are soft on workers' rights. This has led to huge human rights abuses: grim working conditions onboard, no legal rights when arrested, little chance of winning compensation when injured, and being made an easy, regular scapegoat when conditions turn sour for an owner. Is it any wonder, then, that there is a global shortage of well-trained crews? UK-based Drewry Shipping Consultants estimates there is an officer shortfall of 34,000 people at present, which could rise to 83,900 by 2012, assuming current supply levels and fleet growth at 17 per cent.

    The world's shipping community finally acknowledged there was a problem with the status quo of their employees and came together in February 2006 in Geneva at the behest of the International Labour

---

Organization (ILO) to thrash out a landmark seafarers' charter or bill of rights. The resulting Maritime Labour Convention 2006 was hailed as a significant breakthrough in establishing uniform maritime workers' rights.

The convention – also known as the Consolidated Maritime Convention because it brings together and updates more than sixty-five other ILO maritime labour instruments – will provide the world's crews with comprehensive social protection for the first time. It sets minimum requirements for seafarers to work on a ship, with provisions on conditions of employment, accommodation, recreational facilities, food and catering, health, medical care, welfare and social security protection.

Under the new convention, ships that are larger than 500 gross tonnes and engaged in international voyages will be required to carry a Maritime Labour Certificate and a Declaration of Maritime Labour Compliance. Most critically, the convention is enforceable. Ships governed by it will not be allowed to sail by port states without securing certificates proving that they meet key labour, health and safety standards. New provisions for, among others, seafarers' complaints procedures and enhanced port inspections should help to ensure compliance.

The convention directly applies only to ships carrying the flag of a nation state that has ratified it. However, the enforcement provisions contain a 'no more favourable treatment' clause. This means, for example, that a ship flagged by a country that has not ratified the convention could still end up in trouble during a port inspection for falling short of the standards it lays down.

The convention represents the so-called 'fourth pillar' of the international regulatory system for the global maritime industry, alongside the IMO's safety, training and pollution conventions, namely the International Convention for the Safety of Life at Sea (SOLAS), the Standards of Training, Certification and Watchkeeping Convention (STCW) and the International Convention for the Prevention of Pollution from Ships (MARPOL).

Jon Whitlow, secretary of the ITF Seafarers' Section, commented at the conclusion of the Geneva talks:

All too often seafarers' rights are under threat and the essential contribution made by the 'human element' forgotten or ignored.

That's why we welcome this convention. It goes some way to addressing our key concerns about seafarers' working conditions and rights, and acknowledges that a global industry needs global regulation enforced at sea and in the world's ports.

ILO Director-General Juan Somavia said on the same day:

We have made maritime labour history today. We have adopted a Convention that spans continents and oceans, providing a comprehensive labour charter for the world's 1.2 mn or more seafarers and addressing the evolving realities and needs of a sector that handles 90 per cent of the world's trade … What's more, we have established a socio-economic floor to global competition in the maritime sector. This initiative can also provide the impetus and support for similarly innovative and balanced approaches to addressing the need to make globalization fair in other sectors of the world of work.

The convention is expected to come into force by mid-2011, after it has been ratified by thirty ILO member states with a total share of at least 33 per cent of world gross tonnage.

An Unenticing Career Option

Whilst we travelled onboard a VLCC in 2008, Indian seafarers recounted to the authors tales of shocking, inhumane treatment that have largely gone unreported. Take Basra in southern Iraq: US marines there have been forcing all crew members bar the captain to assemble at the prow of the ship where they are handcuffed and guarded by gun-toting soldiers while the ship is loaded. This entails hours standing in the searingly hot, bright sunshine of the Gulf.

Similarly, seafarers often groan when they hear their next rotation includes a call or two at US ports. Pakistani and Bangladeshi seafarers calling at US ports have to have a United States Sea Marshal alongside them at all times while they are in the country. The cost is US$3,000 per day per marshal and the ratio is one marshal per seafarer. If a ship is sailing from the Gulf to the US, Pakistanis will often be replaced in South Africa with other nationals to avoid these excessive costs in America. In the US, shore leave is an enormous hassle. Seafarers have to take the same taxi in and out of the port (a photo of the driver plus licence is taken), so the meter keeps running.

'How is the next generation going to react to the prospect of a career at sea when they hear stories like that?' ranted the master of the tanker *Shinyo Ocean*, which was making its way from Singapore to Taiwan when we boarded. Herein lies the crux of the problem with the current attitude to seafarers. The human resources tap for young cadets with an eye for officer class is being turned off. The continued harsh treatment of crews comes at a time when there are record numbers of ships on order. There are unlikely to be enough officers to control these ships, largely thanks to the increasingly unattractive image seafaring has earned itself.

The global shortage of marine officers is projected nearly to treble to 27,000 by 2015 from about 10,000 now, according to a study by the Baltic and International Maritime Council, or Bimco, the world's largest shipping association. It estimates the global supply of officers at 466,000 against a demand of 476,000. Moreover, the shortage is most acute for tankers.

Table 6.1 **Officer class: top ten countries of origin of officers**

India	46,497
Philippines	46,359
China	42,704
Ukraine	28,908
Turkey	22,091
Russia	21,680
Greece	17,000
UK	14,050
Japan	12,968
Vietnam	10,504

Source: Bimco/International Shipping Federation (ISF) 2005 officer survey

Back in the *Shinyo Ocean*'s master's native India, with 82,000 people at sea the world's second largest source of seafarers after the Philippines, the rapid rise of the economy and the sudden wealth of career options led by IT and outsourcing has knocked the idea of a job at sea far down the pecking order. The idea of being away from home and family for such long periods in this advanced communications era seems anathema to India's youth. There are plenty of easier, less lonely ways to make money nowadays. This is a demographic maturity which has seen officers from developed countries in North America and Western Europe all but disappear in the space of a generation. The world's ship owners, who more often than not hail from developed countries, are at the mercy of people from less developed nations to ensure their ships actually move.

Five years ago the Foreign Owners Representatives and Ship Managers Association, a body representing ship owners and managers operating in India, was overwhelmed with an average of 3,000 applications for 200 jobs. Today, for the same number of jobs, it receives barely 600 applications, a figure that continues to fall. A career at sea is now increasingly perceived as dangerous, dirty and degrading. Moreover, many shudder at the long road ahead before the big wages come in – too much study, too many exams, too much paperwork before the decent earnings kick in.

Of course, the flip-side is that pent-up demand and limited supply have seen wages spiral, up 25 per cent on average in one year alone. A ship's first officer or engineer currently earns about US$2,500 a month. The salaries of captains and chief engineers range from US$8,000 to US$12,000, and on specialised gas tankers can top $20,000. However, with the huge recession that shipping has entered – the worst for at least thirty years – crew wages have now plateaued.

The Epicentre of World Crewing

Meanwhile, in the heart of Manila, on Karaw Street in the historic Malate district, which serves as the noisy epicentre for Philippine seafarer recruitment, there's little overt sign of a shipping downturn. The Philippines provides more than one in four seafarers to merchant ships around the globe and in Japan Filipinos actually crew 70 per cent of all ships. Recruitment ads still adorn huge billboards along the cluttered avenues of the Philippine capital, and the area along Karaw Street by the Luneta Seafarer's Centre is packed with aspiring crew and busy agents getting their 10 per cent. 'It's become like a fish market,' says Captain Andy Malpass, a long-term Manila resident and provider of shipping insurance.

Malpass has observed some similar demographic trends to those in India, including the globalisation of white-collar work which will negatively affect seafarer availability in the future. The nation's minimum wage is 9,000 Philippine Pesos (US$180) a month but the huge rise in outsourcing that has come to the archipelago means many can make 20,000 pesos each month. It is not just call centres but even law firms outsourcing paralegal work, Walt Disney and architects sending storyboards and plans here to draw up. 'You can spot the call centres,' notes Malpass, 'as McDonald's and Starbucks spring up near them.'

This ready cash to be made on home shores is taking away many potential candidates from a career at sea. 'The marketing is simply not there for sea careers,' complains Malpass. Moreover, the press here constantly carries horror stories of mistreatment or calamity hitting Filipinos at sea across the world. John Wood, fleet personnel director of Hong Kong's Wallem Shipmanagement, says that while ratings are not a problem in the Philippines, sourcing the right officer gets harder and harder. 'Quality and quantity and age are the three things of greatest concern for me in the Philippines,' he says. Many officers are now old and life at sea, walking up and down the accommodation block, requires a certain level of fitness, hence Wallem's mandatory treadmill tests. Captain Malpass related how not long ago he came across a claim from a sixty-eight-year-old chief engineer still crewing on ships.

Like India, the Philippines suffers from a very high percentage of cadets who never make the leap beyond second officer. They make their money for a number of years and then head home, open a business with their savings and never go back to sea. Only 8 per cent of officers from East and South East Asia are over fifty years old. Typically, to become a master of a ship would take at least ten years. Now some companies are dangerously rushing the training of employees to fill the gaps in senior ranks.

The one major maritime force that has not suffered, or is unlikely to suffer in the future, from this acute officer shortage is China. Back at the turn of the millennium there were many farsighted shipping companies who began to eye China as a potential source to fill the incoming seafarer shortage, and yet China has not emerged as a genuine international force on the world's merchant fleet. Why? The number of Chinese seafarers has grown massively in the past decade as have the training facilities and maritime colleges up and down the Chinese coast. However, the vast majority have been drafted onboard the mainland's own merchant fleet. And, unlike other nations who face an inevitable demographic time bomb for their crewing numbers to implode, China's labour resources are nearly limitless in that once the seam of coastal workers becomes too expensive or opts for a different career option there are hundreds of millions of keen poorer applicants raring to sign up from inland China. Many of them already have some shipping know-how thanks to the huge volumes of traffic plying China's inland waterways and rivers, principally the Yangtze.

Accidents Will Happen

The increased paperwork now demanded by port authorities around the world, especially after the September 11 attacks in the US, has increasingly made senior officers prisoners at their desks. This combined with an industry willing to cut corners on manpower to keep its ships moving has resulted in a clear escalation of accidents in recent years. 'We believe that the rapid growth of the world fleet coupled with a severe shortage of experienced seafarers is one key factor [*in the escalation of maritime accidents*],' read a 2007 report from the North of England P&I (Protection and Indemnity) Club, a company that insures a significant percentage of the world merchant fleet.

Det Norske Veritas (DNV), a Norwegian-based leading classification society whose role is to certify that industrial contraptions, principally ships, are safe, conducted a survey in 2008 that showed losses from navigational accidents continued to rise at an alarming rate. Accidents doubled from 2003 to 2008, due to a combination of the continued growth of the world fleet and a shortage of officers with the right skills, according to DNV Maritime's Principal Safety Consultant Torkel Soma. DNV's statistics show that a ship is twice as likely to be involved in a serious accident today compared to only five years ago. DNV Maritime South East Asia's Regional Manager Helge Kjeøy, added: 'The main factors explaining the negative developments over the past few years are that the undersupply of crew worldwide results in reduced experience and that the high commercial pressure results in a high workload.'[11]

So then the growing scourge of piracy that has led to crew murders, the increasing maltreatment of seafarers, greater job opportunities back home and more and more shipping accidents are all casting a pall over crew recruitment at a time when projections for the next four years show that shipyards are set to deliver more new ships than ever before. Vijay Rangroo, managing director of Singapore-based MTM Ship Management, was blunt in his assessment of the situation when speaking at a conference in Singapore: 'We are a dinosaur industry when it comes to the development of human capital.'[12]

There is, however, growing awareness within the industry that shipping's lowly public image must change to get more people signing up for a career at sea. Many projects are under way across the world to boost shipping's aura. The European Commission, for instance, announced the 2010 launch of a three-year €3 mn programme aimed at increasing public awareness and boosting recruitment that has received the support of many leading shipping organisations. Moreover, 2010 has been designated the Year of the Seafarer by the UN body charged with overseeing shipping, the IMO.

The worry is that all these efforts might be too little too late.

CHAPTER SEVEN

Flags of Convenience

28 May 2009 – Ulan Bator, Mongolia

Think of landlocked Mongolia and the first images that are likely to spring to mind are of yaks and yurts, Genghis and Kublai Khan. Barren arid plateaus encircled by Russia and China – twixt the bear and the dragon – with the Gobi Desert stretching through much of its western regions. It is a country with little primacy on the international stage, one so spread out and rural that general elections take weeks to conclude to enable nomads on horseback to flock from far and wide. Just three million people live on one million square miles of land. Mongolia is more than six times as large as the UK.

The men are huge and strapping – the world champion sumo wrestler is a Mongolian. Most outsiders would be hard pushed to name any city in this central Asian nation other than the capital Ulan Bator. UB, as regular visitors like to call it, is a homage to all the worst tenets of Communist architecture – a vision in grey, squat concrete.

Over the years we have been visiting UB it has changed a lot. From an invariably cold city of seeming commercial inertia, Stalinist architecture and few entertainment options it has become an invariably cold city of entrepreneurial buzz, teeming construction and a diverse nightlife. The discerning visitor might be able to spot a couple of sushi bars that have popped up in recent years. Bravery is needed to step inside such establishments, however, given that the nearest oceans lie more than 600 miles away. And yet Mongolia, the largest landlocked country on earth, has two seaworthy claims. First, by dint of millions of yen from Tokyo it consistently casts a crucial vote in favour of whale hunting. Second, and more pertinently for the purposes of this

127

book, it controls a fleet of more than a hundred ships via its 2003-founded shipping registry.

It was a curious bureaucratic accident that brought this land of nomadic herders into contact with the potential riches to be made from looking after vessels. A young male student known only as Ganbataar won a scholarship to study fish farming in the Soviet Union twenty-five years ago. The apparatchik filling out his application form mistakenly put Ganbataar down for course 1012, rather than 1013.

As Ganbataar will happily recount, that bureaucratic error took him from fish farming to deep-sea fishing. After graduating he went to work with the seven-man Mongolian Navy, which patrols the country's biggest lake, Hovsgol. The lone ship in the navy was a Soviet-era tugboat that was brought bit by bit over the steppes, assembled and launched in 1938. Following the collapse of Communism, Ganbaatar wrote Mongolia's new maritime law, which was promulgated in 1999.

Four years later the Mongolia Ship Registry was launched from a dusty office on UB's Genghis Khan Avenue and assisted commercially by a Singaporean firm, Sovereign Ventures, a company that had just relinquished control of the Cambodian shipping register following numerous scandals, the final curtain coming from a large cocaine haul on one of its ships. Sovereign Ventures is headed by Captain Chong Koy Sen, who is also a major shareholder with Korasia Shipping and Trading. Korasia operates ships for the Democratic People's Republic of Korea and, through Sovereign Ventures, explores for oil and gas in North Korea. The Hermit Kingdom, as the land of Kim Jong-il is often referred to, had used the Cambodian flag to register many of its ships. When Chong's contract with Phnom Penh was ripped up and he headed to Ulan Bator, Kim Jong-il's fleet was among the first to sign up for the red, blue and gold flag of Mongolia, thus helping the rogue state avoid the eye of the US Navy.

Mongolia 'is indicative of the larger, growing trend of the weakening of the nation state on the high seas', William Langewiesche, author of The Outlaw Sea: A World of Freedom, Chaos, and Crime, told the New York Times. In the same 2004 article, many ancient ships registered with the flag were reported to have perished, with much of the flagged fleet described as 'sinking time bombs for the sailors'. The *then prime minister of Mongolia, Nambaryn Enkhbayar, conceded. 'Unfortunately, there were a few Mongolian-flag ships that sank.'[1]*

A glance at the Mongolian flag's Singaporean developed website explains its raison d'être: a shield for less scrupulous ship owners to cut costs covertly. Its brochure makes plain the registry is cheap, can sign anyone up within twenty-four hours online, offers owners zero taxes, and does not make a uniform minimum demand for the number of crew that should be on board a ship. Mongolia, and its forerunner Cambodia, are but two of many more obscure backwaters offering to take rust buckets under their wing, turning a blind eye to best practice and bringing the whole shipping industry into disrepute – formally known as the provision of flags of convenience.

The Beginning of the Open Registry System

The phrase for these types of operation is 'flags of convenience' (FoC). A ship is defined as flying one of these flags if it is registered in a foreign country, 'for purposes of reducing operating costs or avoiding government regulations'.

The term was first coined in the 1950s though its practice goes back to just after World War I. Where a ship is registered determines the laws under which the ship is required to operate. A typical ship of 70,000 dwt will pay around US$20,000 for a flag per year. The huge revenue potential to be had from the world's approximately 50,000-vessel merchant fleet, combined with the limited infrastructure of small, less developed nations, has allowed third parties to step in and operate certain new flags on behalf of nations. Making a profit is the primary objective for these third-party corporations whatever the flowery marketing blurb of their brochures might say about quality. This has led to a dark subjugation of the maritime world, where profit obstructs best practice and ultimately costs lives and the environment.

In 1919 the *Belen Quezada* became the first foreign-owned ship to register with the Panamanian flag. In the ensuing years more American ships followed to Panama and Honduras. Flagging overseas helped avoid the restrictions in place during the Prohibition era. By the late 1940s there was growing dissatisfaction with the Panama flag's operations and an American firm set up the Liberian Registry in 1948. Other flags of convenience, or open registers as they are often described, opened up for business.

Currently, the three largest ship registries are open registers: namely Panama, Liberia and the Bahamas. All of these are judged by international safety organisations as 'white-listed' flags, indicating above-average safety performance. Nevertheless, these flags have had their fair share of bad press. The Bahamas and Liberia were the flags responsible for two of the worst oil spills ever, the *Prestige* and the *Amoco Cadiz*.

Table 7.1 **Leading twenty shipping registers globally by tonnage, 2008**

Country	Gross shipping tonnage (mn)
Panama	173
Liberia	79
Bahamas	47
Marshall Islands	38
Singapore	37
Hong Kong	36
Greece	36
Malta	27
China (PRC)	26
USA	20
Cyprus	19
Norway	15
UK	14
Italy	13
South Korea	13
Germany	13
Japan	13
Bermuda	10
India	9
Denmark	9

Source: *Lloyd's Register/Fairplay*

Flags of Convenience

At present, more than half of the world's merchant tonnage is registered with flags of convenience. The status of FoCs has been further muddied in recent years by the decision of many nations to set up secondary registers to compete against the open registers. This sees, for instance, the Isle of Man offering competitive rates and minimal manning requirements to better compete with its big brother red ensign flag, the UK. South Korea, Norway and Denmark all have secondary flags – more are likely.

Table 7.2 **Leading twenty actual ship owners by country by percentage of world fleet, 2008**

Country	Per cent of world fleet
Greece	17.4
Japan	15.1
Germany	8.7
China (PRC)	7.2
Norway	5.0
USA	4.9
Hong Kong	4.6
South Korea	3.3
UK	2.7
Singapore	2.6
Taiwan (ROC)	2.5
Denmark	2.2
Russian Federation	1.9
Italy	1.6
India	1.5
Switzerland	1.3
Belgium	1.3
Saudi Arabia	1.2
Turkey	1.1
Iran	1.0

Source: *Lloyd's Register/Fairplay*

131

The Case Against FoCs

One of the most consistently critical voices against the rise of open registers has been the International Transport Workers' Federation (ITF). 'FoCs provide a means of avoiding labour regulation in the country of ownership, and become a vehicle for paying low wages and forcing long hours of work and unsafe working conditions,' the ITF maintains. 'Since FoC ships have no real nationality, they are beyond the reach of any single national seafarers' trade union.'[2] The Federation also accuses such ships of having low safety standards and no construction requirements.

Another regular broadside fired at owners who flag outside their native land is that they are tax dodging, an issue likely to grow with the continuing crackdown on non-domiciled individuals. A further aspect rarely discussed is how much these third-party corporations who look after a registry for a nation actually give back to the country. For instance, despite repeated requests, International Registries Inc., which used to look after the Liberian flag from its Virginia headquarters and now presides over the Marshall Islands FoC, refuses to reveal what its split is with the South Pacific archipelago.

Ship owners fire back that if they were forced to flag in their home countries the price of world trade would soar. Many national registers have plenty of restrictive priorities, such as a demand that crews hail from the home country, even that ships are built in the home nation. FoCs allow owners the freedom to choose where to buy their ships, where to source crew and seek finance, and by extension make the movement of cargo that bit cheaper.

The ITF keeps a list of thirty-two registries it considers to be FoC registries. In developing the list, the ITF considers 'ability and willingness of the flag state to enforce international minimum social standards on its vessels', the 'degree of ratification and enforcement of ILO Conventions and Recommendations' and 'safety and environmental record'. On the ITF list is another landlocked nation, Bolivia.

Table 7.3 **Where to find a flag of convenience**

The following thirty-two countries have been declared FoCs by the ITF's Fair Practices Committee (a joint committee of ITF seafarers' and dockers' unions), which runs the ITF campaign against FoCs:

Antigua and Barbuda	Gibraltar (UK)
Bahamas	Honduras
Barbados	Jamaica
Belize	Lebanon
Bermuda (UK)	Liberia
Bolivia	Malta
Burma	Marshall Islands (USA)
Cambodia	Mauritius
Cayman Islands	Mongolia
Comoros	Netherlands Antilles
Cyprus	North Korea
Equatorial Guinea	Panama
French International Ship Register (FIS)	São Tomé and Príncipe
	St Vincent
German International Ship Register (GIS)	Sri Lanka
	Tonga
Georgia	Vanuatu

Source: ITF

The Federation's FoC campaign, which has been ongoing for more than half a century, has tried and failed to eliminate FoCs. It continues to attack sub-standard shipping and looks to seek ITF-acceptable standards on all ships irrespective of flag, using all the political, industrial and legal means at the Federation's disposal. Wherever it can, the ITF highlights corruption and substandard practice. This has seen some significant exposés over the years.

'A first officer's certificate to navigate a ship and deputise for captain. No training, no skills. Price, US$4,500.' David Cockroft, the ITF's secretary general, sent shockwaves through the shipping business when he bought that certificate in Panama in 2001 to show corruption in shipping registries.

Continuing a theme that is prevalent throughout this book, the ITF states that seafarers are 'an invisible labour force'. There are more than 2,000 seafarer deaths a year at sea, the majority of which take place on board open registered vessels. Likewise, serious injuries occur more often than not on board FoC ships. Crew members and their families stand little chance of winning compensation on their own. This is partly because of the arcane, hidden nature of ship owning: following an accident, a series of brass plaques often obfuscates who the real owners are. By selecting an open register owners can often choose the cheapest crews available and not worry about working conditions in the knowledge that the country where the ship is registered has weak trade unions.

Sinking Ships

Even after dramatic disasters where attempting to unravel complex company structures has hindered state investigations, the FoC system still continues. For instance, ten years have passed since one of Europe's most infamous tanker disasters – the *Erika*. The 1975-built *Erika*, an ancient (in shipping terms) 37,000-tonne ship registered under the Maltese flag, was booked as a bargain-basement charter from France to Italy. The vessel was so cheap because of its age. Despite being at the end of its normal shelf life, it was still able to trade thanks to its flag's generous rules.

On 8 December 1999 the *Erika* set off from Dunkirk, passing through the English Channel en route to Sicily, carrying more than 30,000 tonnes of viscous heavy fuel oil. On entering the Bay of Biscay the tanker hit a heavy storm. The weather worsened and by the middle of the afternoon of 11 December the ship started to list to starboard by 10 to 12 degrees. The ship's hull was showing cracks, water seeped onboard and the ship gradually began to shed layers of steel like a peeled onion.

The crew, led by Captain Karun Mathur, were helpless. At 2.08 p.m. the captain issued a mayday emergency call. Having contacted his bosses ashore, however, he curiously rescinded this mayday despite the fact that the cracks in the hull 130 feet below him were clearly getting larger and larger. Towards 6 a.m. on 12 December the *Erika* issued a second mayday call, sixteen hours after the first, the ship now awash with oil and waves. Rescue operations began 40 nautical miles off the Breton coast amidst winds gusting at almost 63 miles per hour and 26-foot waves. At 8.10 a.m. the oil tanker broke in half. 'The ship folded in two like a book closing,' Captain Mathur would later tell investigators.[3] Thankfully, all twenty-six crew members were rescued.

Aerial photographs documented this stunning tragic demise as the rusty red hull sunk below the surface. Thousands of tonnes of oil began to seep from the *Erika*'s cargo tanks. Britanny, famed throughout Europe for its rugged untouched coastline, faced an ominously long oil blanket washing up to its shores. Soon images of birds covered in slick black oil were being beamed across the world. In total some 20,000 tonnes of thick fuel oil gushed out of the stricken ship, washing up along 250 miles of Breton coastline. Indignation ran high among the French public. Answers were needed fast – who had owned this hulk and how could it have been allowed to trade?

The investigations got under way. They would be long and frustrating due to shipping's many corporate dead ends created by open registers. The *Erika* was one of eight sister ships built more than twenty-five years previously in Japan. The vessels were cheap, partially thanks to the fact that 10 per cent less steel was used in their construction. Three of *Erika*'s sisters have suffered major structural damage.

French investigators became increasingly irate as their pursuit of the ship's owner led them to one off-shore company after another. They described this commercial fog as 'unacceptable' and 'against the public interest'. The paper trail led through seven different countries. It is common practice for each and every single ship owned under an FoC to be made into a single ship company, thus limiting liability to just one ship in the event of an accident. Having pulled the corporate string through many labyrinthine mazes, the investigators eventually found the owner of the *Erika*.

The ship was an FoC vessel that had changed ownership several times, was controlled by a Malta-based brass-plaque ship owner and had undergone several changes of classification. The cargo on board, owned by the oil company Total Bermuda, was bound for the ENEL (Italy's Ente Nazionale per l'Energia eLettrica) oil-fired power station at Livorno on the western edge of Tuscany. At the time, the ship was on a single voyage charter arranged via Petrian Shipbrokers of London on behalf of the London office of the world's fourth largest oil and gas company, TotalFina. The *Erika* had been re-let for this voyage by Amarship, based in Lugano in Switzerland, acting as an agent for Nassau-based Selmont International, to which the vessel was on time charter.

It became even more confusing. The technical management and crewing of the *Erika* was entrusted to Panship Management of Ravenna in Italy's Emilia-Romagna region. The legal owner of the *Erika*, since its acquisition in 1996, was the single-ship Maltese company Tevere Shipping Company Ltd, although the ultimate beneficial ownership of the vessel was eventually traced back to its London-based ship owner, the Italian Giuseppe Savarese. The purchase of the ship was reportedly secured via a loan obtained from the Bank of Scotland.

In the meantime, again as is so common in shipping accidents (see chapter 6, 'The Criminalisation of Crews'), the authorities had been quick to arrest the captain. Only after a week was he released on bail. Since the disaster, it had emerged that the inspections undertaken by its classification society, Italy's Registro Italiano Navale (RINA) in Genoa, oil companies and the flag took place without all cargo and ballast tanks having been fully gas-freed. The limited extent of these inspections helps to explain how the loss of the vessel could have occurred.

The willingness of the flag to cut corners to please customers shocked many. However, the international legislation that followed in *Erika*'s wake did nothing to clamp down on FoCs or the increasingly competitive classification scene. Classification societies typically receive between 1 and 1.5 per cent of a ship's value in return for certifying a ship is safe. These societies have become enormously competitive and one (Bureau Veritas of France) has even listed on the stock market, bringing into question whether a society's primary objective is ensuring safety and good shipping practice or profits and market share. In the wake of the *Erika*, the only international legislation that came into place was the phase-out of single-hulled tankers by 2010 in favour of ships with a double skin. A voluntary code to improve transparency and best practice among tanker owners was put forward. But voluntary codes are only good if they are uniformly accepted. Bad practice has persisted.

The twenty-six-year-old *Prestige* was another single-hulled tanker whose stern heading down towards the ocean floor would provide news channels with more gripping disaster footage three years later and bring shipping's murky ownership rules into the spotlight once again. The 81,000 dwt ship ran into difficulties during a storm. It was carrying 77,000 tonnes of two different grades of heavy fuel oil. When on 13 November 2002 one of its twelve tanks burst off the coast of Galicia in north-western Spain, local authorities denied the ship access to harbours, thereby forcing the captain to head north towards France. The French in turn gave the tanker short shrift and the vessel became a political football. The now desperate captain headed south towards Portugal, desperate to dock. The Portuguese Navy were on hand, however, to deny access to the ship and force it back out to sea.

Like the *Erika* before it, the *Prestige* had been built at minimal cost using as little steel as possible. The storm continued to ravage the ship. A 40-foot section of the starboard hull broke off, oil gushing from the gash. In the meantime, the world's press had a field day. 'Tanker adrift and spewing black gold,' read one headline while another sensationally wrote 'Russian mafia behind oil time bomb.' Finally at around 8.00 a.m. on 19 November, the ship split in half, becoming a semi-submerged V shape. It sank completely the same afternoon, releasing over 20 mn gallons of oil into the sea. The oil tanker was reported to be about 160 miiles from the Spanish coast at that time. An earlier oil slick had already reached the coast. The Greek captain of the *Prestige* was taken into custody and investigations got under way in Spain into what would become one of the worst marine environmental disasters of all time.

Like their French counterparts a couple of years previously, Spanish investigators were flabbergasted at the complex web of ownership relating to the *Prestige*. As Will Hutton wrote in the *Observer*:

This was a vessel chartered by the Swiss-based subsidiary of a Russian conglomerate registered in the Bahamas, owned by a Greek through Liberia and given a certificate of seaworthiness by the Americans. When it refuelled, it stood off the port of Gibraltar to avoid the chance of inspection. Every aspect of its operations was calculated to avoid tax, ownership obligations and regulatory scrutiny.[4]

The ship was over twenty-five years old, an age when most decent flag states pension off tankers to scrapyards. However, it had been classified as safe by both the flag state, the Bahamas, and its class society, the American Bureau of Shipping in Houston, Texas. And yet, once again, in the wake of the *Prestige*'s demise no international action was taken to make flag states more uniform in their dismissal of sub-standard tonnage. The only regulation that came from the accident was a demand to increase the thickness of steel on the hulls of ships.

Market Forces at Play

In 2008–2009 two issues occurred that have both boosted and diminished the attractiveness of FoCs around the world. The first is the financial crisis, which has led shipping to its worst economic position for a generation with many ship owners facing the abyss. This has seen ship owners everywhere look for every means possible to cut costs, playing into the hands of the open registers. Writing in industry journal *Lloyd's List*, Jon Whitlow, the ITF's seafarers' section secretary, noted:

> The need to establish accepted and acceptable conditions onboard the world's ships is still undermined by the patchwork of ownership and flags, especially those that tout for business by undercutting their competitors in oversight, inspection and crew costs … In fact it is the globalised nature of cut-throat competition and cost cutting that makes ever more necessary the protection and level playing field that the FoC system cannot provide.[5]

Ships are being abandoned around the world, crews effectively marooned, unpaid and left to fend for themselves. Ships that are with an FoC are unlikely to have a significant trade union to protect those onboard.

However, the one deterrent for ship owners opting for open registers in recent months has been the rise of piracy, especially off the Gulf of Aden and around the Horn of Africa. Reverting back to national registries with credible naval assets provides owners with some assurance while transiting these increasingly treacherous waters. But this is a small blip. The rise and rise of the flag of convenience appears unstoppable until international condemnation reaches breaking point. At the moment, those fighting hard against the system are regulators from developed nations led by the EU. Less developed nations like the money from the open registers to care too much about the odd oil spill.

Box 7.1 A Very Dirty Flag: Cambodia

The rise and fall of the Cambodia flag – the forerunner to the Mongolian open registry – is an outrageous tale that once again shows clearly the dangers of shipping being left to its own devices. In 1994 the South East Asian nation set up its own registry, the Cambodian Shipping Corporation (CSC). After a slow start with just sixteen foreign ships onboard by the end of year one, growth snowballed at this the most open of open registers. Prior to its winding up in 2002 it had as many as a thousand vessels on its books.

All ships were welcome regardless of who owned them, what they were trading or their condition. Prices for registration were fantastically low. And, unlike among its peers, registration could be done super fast – within twenty-four hours – all online thanks to the Singapore company, Sovereign Ventures, charged with overseeing the flag.

The flag became a magnet for illegal practices. Cigarette-smuggling operations were discovered near Crete and Albania; during the oil embargo of Iraq, oil was smuggled out of that country; human trafficking and prostitution operations were discovered near Japan and Crete; and, of course, there was drug trafficking. It was also the flag of choice for arms smuggling.

Among CSC's major clients were North Korean firms. One North Korean ship, the *So San*, flying the Cambodian flag, was stopped by US and Spanish naval forces in the Indian Ocean. The *So San's* manifest stated that it was transporting cement to Yemen, but an examination revealed fifteen Scud missiles with fifteen conventional warheads, twenty-three tanks of nitric acid rocket propellant and eighty-five drums of unidentified chemicals all hidden beneath the bags of cement.

When asked about CSC's alleged illegal operations, Ahamd Yahya of the Cambodian Ministry of Public Works and Transport told the shipping industry journal *Fairplay*: 'We don't know or care who owns the ships or whether they're doing "white" or "black" business ... it is not our concern.'[6]

The registry was a centre of sub-standard tonnage with more than one in ten ships on its books having been involved in one incident or another, leading to the deaths of hundreds of seafarers. A worldwide clamour against this den of iniquity grew and grew, with the ITF stating in the summer of 2002, 'The world should join us in demanding that Cambodia shut down this sleazy and pestilent offshore registration. How many more people have to die in incidents involving Cambodian-flagged vessels, or its ships detained for illegal activities, before something is actually done about it?'[7]

In 2002 the Greek-owned, but Cambodian-registered, *Winner* was seized by French forces and discovered to be smuggling a large amount of cocaine. Shortly after this embarrassment the Cambodian government, headed by Hun Sen, revoked the Singaporean company's control of CSC. Sovereign Ventures would shift its allegiance to Mongolia. The Cambodian flag is now run by a South Korean company.

North Korea moved its ships to Mongolia and other flags with equally scant regard to procedure. This has resulted in countless ship arrests for the Hermit Kingdom, including the 2003 seizure of a North Korean freighter by Australian authorities who found US$50 mn worth of heroin onboard.

The ship in question, the *Pong Su*, was registered in the small South Pacific island nation of Tuvalu, a place that derives capital from ship registration and web-domain registrations for its .tv suffix. It seems that those who wish to carry out nefarious activities on the high seas can usually find a compliant FoC without too much trouble.

In Black and White

The Paris Memorandum of Understanding on Port State Control issued its 2008 rankings in June 2009, based on the results of thousands of inspections across Europe and the North Atlantic, placing Bermuda at the top of the 'white list'. The inspections of thousands of ships divides vessels into three lists – white for good, grey for questionable and black for urgent attention. The UK had jumped two places on the previous year, coming in at number three, with France in second place. Leading flags of convenience such as the Marshall Islands and Liberia also made the cut, while the US has been relegated to grey-list standing.

The black list of flags that face increased scrutiny include long-standing poor performers such as the largest register in the world, Panama, along with North Korea, Bolivia and Albania. This year they are joined by Libya, Moldova and Dominica. Belize, meanwhile, has failed to achieve its long-standing goal of shaking off the black-list tag. All told, the white list now numbers forty-one countries, three more than last year, while there are twenty-one black-list flags, two more than previously.

FoCs remain big business for some.

CHAPTER EIGHT

Green Shipping?

Tuesday 7 October 2008 – The South China Sea, off the coast of Vietnam

On a clear evening as the sun sets 'Monkey Island' (the name given to the uppermost deck onboard a supertanker) is one of the best places to see the deadly fumes that billow out from a ship's funnel. Looking aft the haze distorts the horizon, the view is altered as if one is wearing special yellow Polaroid lenses. The otherwise stunningly clear landless view is blurred by the noxious output of the 50-foot- high funnel.

A hundred and thirty feet below, deep in the hull of the ship, the pistons thunder at deafening volumes; the engine room – the size of an Olympic swimming pool – is infernally hot. Ships of VLCC class will typically burn through 1.5 tonnes of bunker fuel an hour, producing annual fuel bills in excess of US$4 mn. Standing on deck watching the thick exhaust froth out of the funnel, it seems amazing that shipping's rather grey-green credentials have so far not been the subject of stronger international scrutiny.

Glancing down to the lapping waves, there's another eye-opener – the vast volumes of garbage littering our oceans. Here, despite there being more than 1,000 nautical miles to the nearest strip of coastline, one of the few constants on our voyage has been the sad sight of trash floating in the otherwise pristine seas – plastic bags, kitchen waste, beer cans. It is as if some errant householder has just tipped their rubbish bin straight into the sea. There are fines in place for anyone caught littering the oceans, yet this age-old practice has been hard to counter, let alone police when it takes place so far away from public view. It is out at sea, such as here high up on Monkey Island, the wind riffling down from the north, that you get to appreciate the true vastness of planet earth. Yet on major trade lanes, trash, especially plastic, ensures that rare is the moment when you can genuinely not see anything man-made washing past.

A June 2006 United Nations environmental programme report estimated that there are an average of 46,000 pieces of plastic debris floating on or near the surface of every square mile of ocean. Shipping is by no means responsible for all this waste, but it certainly contributes. Today debris in the oceans is a major threat to the marine environment. It is estimated that each year it kills more than a million sea birds, as well as 100,000 marine animals and turtles through ingestion and entanglement.[1]

Fig. 8.1 A tanker's funnel belches emissions

One traditional reason given for ships' failure to discharge their waste to shore has been inadequate provision of port waste reception facilities (PRFs). While this may still play some part, low levels of usage in ports that have excellent PRF provision suggest that the real reason for dumping at sea is often to save on the fees that ports normally charge for the use of such facilities. Ships can save these fees and dump at sea with little chance of being caught. Authorities are trying to put in place a global ban on any form of garbage dumping. How this can be enforced remains unknown. Preventing the dumping of trash at sea is just one item on shipping's green agenda.

Stratospherically Worse than Aviation

Eighty-seven thousand. That's the number of people that will die each year by 2012 from the pollution belching out of all the ships trading around the world, according to a study by the American Chemical Society.[2] As many as 60,000 are already dying each year from the deadly cocktail of lethal pollutants produced by funnels across the world's oceans, according to the University of Stockholm. They may not get the attention of air travel, but ships pollute on a vast scale.

Shipping has so far ducked under the radar of the environmental regulators, but its emissions have soared 85 per cent since 1990. It managed to avoid the constraints of the Kyoto Protocol. Like so much else in the maritime business, the concept of 'out of sight, out of mind' has shielded shipping from intergovernmental green regulations. People regularly see jet-plane vapour trails across the skies and sit in traffic jams watching the exhaust of the car in front but they rarely, if ever, see ship-funnel emissions. For years shipping has hidden behind the smoggy cloud of the air industry, which has taken the brunt of criticism from environmentalists. Airports are more media friendly targets for campaigners than ports; airline chief executives are more visible than ship owners; and few people travel anywhere on commercial ships these days.

Now, however, the knives are out. Shipping's greenhouse gas contributions are under the spotlight like never before. The shipping industry entered a frenzied rush to come up with a common position ahead of what was meant to be the crucial international gathering in Copenhagen in December 2009 to thrash out a resolution on reducing shipping's environmental footprint. 'Green shipping' is now an industry buzz term.

In 2008 the mainstream media caught up with the long sooty trail left behind by the world's merchant shipping fleet. In February of that year a leaked UN study revealed the dark truth about ship emissions.[3] The report (using data gathered from the International Maritime Organization) showed shipping was responsible for nearly twice aviation's emissions, accounting for 1.12 bn tonnes of CO_2 emissions in 2007 or around 3 per cent of all global emissions of the main greenhouse gases. Moreover, the UN report warned that the world's growing merchant fleet would inevitably result in the industry becoming the fifth largest source of man-made CO_2 after cars, housing, agriculture and industry. Shipping's emission footprint would rise by at least 30 per cent by 2020, the report posited.

Up until then the UN's Intergovernmental Panel on Climate Change (IPCC) thought shipping emissions amounted to no more than 400 mn tonnes a year, three times less than the revised figure. What's more, over 25 mn tonnes of nitrous oxides (NOx) are emitted by ships, as well as sulphur oxide and particulate matter. Dr Rajendra Pachauri, chair of the IPCC, said as the report came to light:

> This is a clear failure of the system. The shipping industry has so far escaped publicity. It has been left out of the climate change discussion. I hope [*shipping emissions*] will be included in the next UN agreement. It would be a cop-out if it was not. It tells me that we have been ineffective at tackling climate change so far.[4]

Pachauri's feelings became reality. The backlash against shipping subsequently went into overdrive. At roughly the same time it was revealed that the shipping and oil exploration activities of the Danish firm AP Moller-Maersk emitted up to 50 mn tonnes of CO_2 a year – as much as the whole of Denmark. However, this doesn't let other forms of transport off the hook: as the tables below show, while shipping's total carbon footprint is immense, in per-km terms shipping is far less environmentally damaging than air or road transport. But the problem of environmentally damaging shipping will not go away. There are no alternatives in oil transportation: millions of barrels of oil are never going to be moved from the Middle East to China by either road or air. Ships will remain the primary transport system for oil.

The environmental pressure group Oceana likes to point out regularly that the shipping industry pumps out as much CO_2 as all the cars in America put together while Arthur Bowring, the managing director of the Hong Kong Shipowners Association (HKSOA) maintains, 'The environment will be the largest single issue that our industry will have to face over the coming years.' Bowring's job is to look after the interests of Hong Kong's ship owners, a powerful collective, who account for around 3 per cent of the global shipping fleet. His organisation, along with the International Association of Independent Tanker Owners (INTERTANKO), the global independent tanker owners' association, has been the most vocal on environmental issues in recent years. 'We burn crap on our ships,' concedes Bowring, 'The end of the refining cycle, the residue; one step up from the asphalt you put on roads.'[5]

This fuel, known as 'bunker fuel', is sold to ship owners at a discount of close to US$20 a barrel, and refiners believe that this is a 'win-win' situation, where owners get cheap fuel and hence improve their operating margins while the major oil corporations get rid of the rubbish they cannot sell anywhere else. This residual bunker fuel is a heavy, viscous fluid that needs heating to between 130 to 140° C and has to be purified extensively before use. The sulphur content varies according to the crude stock, but globally it has an average of about 2.7 per cent. Just about every commercial ship uses it.

Table 8.1 CO_2 emissions per km from shipping, aircraft and road haulage

Mode of Transport	CO_2 (grams per ton per km)
Cargo vessel over 8,000 dwt	15
Cargo vessel 2,000–8,000 dwt	21
Heavy truck with trailer	50
Air freight (747-400)	540

Source: NTM (Swedish Network for Transport and the Environment)

Table 8.2 **Comparative air emissions by major modes of commercial transportation**

Grams emitted (ton per km)	Air	Road	Sea
Nitrogen oxides	3.79	0.80	0.54
Hydrocarbons	0.60	0.07	0.02
Particulates	N/A	0.07	0.01
Carbon monoxide	2.60	0.12	0.03
Sulphur dioxide	0.60	0.33	0.36

Source: NTM (Swedish Network for Transport and the Environment)
Note: based on a 747-200 flying 1,200 km, a medium-sized truck and a vessel of 2,000–8,000 dwt

Dithering while the World Rages

The United Nations body charged with overseeing shipping, the IMO, estimates that shipping emissions could increase by 150–250 per cent by the year 2050. And yet this institution is struggling to find universal common ground among the world's shipping bodies to enforce a path towards greener trade. The longer the industry dithers, the more likely its decisions are to be made for it from above. The clock is ticking.

While both shipping and aviation were exempted from the 1997 Kyoto Protocol (which came into force in 2005), they are unlikely to be left out in the future. The UN Climate Change Conference held in Copenhagen in December 2009 was meant to draw up a successor to Kyoto, and include aviation and shipping in its deliberations. Shipping needs to be seen to be united in its bid to reduce its footprint or else the UN and the EU will clamp down, the latter likely to include the sector in its regional greenhouse gas emissions trading system. At the IMO-convened Marine Environment Protection Committee (MEPC) meeting in July 2009, a gathering aimed at framing IMO policy for Copenhagen, opinion remained too divided to deliver any concrete positions.

Since 1983 the shipping industry has been regulated for environmental matters through the International Convention for the Prevention of Pollution from Ships, or MARPOL for short. Air emissions come under Annex VI of the Convention. Annex VI came into force in May 2005, some seven and a half years after its adoption and seventeen years after the work on drafting it started. So, it was already out of date. Its contentious review is continuing. Annex VI sets a global sulphur cap for fuel oil of 4.5 per cent. Then, in October 2008, a body of the IMO unanimously voted in a package of new measures to reduce harmful emissions from ships, which has been ratified by fifty-three countries, representing approximately 82 per cent of the gross tonnage of the world's merchant shipping fleet. The global sulphur cap will be gradually reduced from the current 4.5 per cent to 0.5 per cent in 2020. In January 2012 the sulphur cap will drop to 3.5 per cent.

Additionally, since 2005, the IMO has developed a series of energy efficiency indices both for new ships and vessels already in operation. It has also come up with a ship energy management plan which incorporates guidance on best practice in areas including voyage planning, optimisation of speed and power and ship and cargo handling. These developments have proved uncontroversial and have been widely accepted by the industry. However, deciding on a market-based mechanism has divided the industry down the middle. The UK Chamber of Shipping has proposed a global and open emissions trading scheme for shipping using the IMO indices as the basis for benchmarking individual ships. The scheme is backed by the UK government and the World Wildlife Fund (WWF). Ships would be allocated a carbon-emission budget in an initial benchmarking exercise, which would recognise existing investment in more emission-efficient tonnage/operation under a cap representing the overall reduction target. One of the loudest proponents of this scheme has been Jan Kopernicki, vice-president of the UK's Chamber of Shipping and vice-president of shipping for the oil giant Shell. He told *Seatrade*, a leading industry journal, in 2009 that this mechanism is the best option available as it is sustainable in the long term: 'that is crucial when discriminating amongst options'.[6] And yet the idea has not received universal acclaim. A significant group would prefer to see a tax on bunkers (or a carbon tax) that would go towards a 'superfund' to stimulate innovation. Proponents of the latter idea claim that, unlike a complex trading scheme, a bunker tax is simple. With little sign of a breakthrough, a third way has been suggested – a hybrid levy/trading scheme, whereby the taxes would go to an international body that would then trade it on the international carbon market.

At MEPC in July 2009 no resolutions were agreed, and only voluntary schemes to improve ship design and onboard operations were agreed upon, leaving green groups rightly seething. Lambasting the MEPC meeting for failing to come up with anything meaningful, organisations such as Oceana and the WWF UK issued a joint statement in which they cited a study that suggested global carbon emissions should not exceed 7.2 bn metric tonnes in 2050 to keep warming below 2° C. 'Business-as-usual' emissions from shipping will eat up 38 per cent to 50 per cent of total allowable emissions by 2050, they suggested. The statement attacked the IMO for having deliberated on emissions for twelve years now without any major breakthrough. Two years alone were devoted to developing market-based instruments, such as an emissions trading scheme, but the efforts were muted due to pressures from China, Saudi Arabia and South Africa, and little resistance from European supporters, according to the statement.

The statement's authors also noted that any efforts to reduce emissions currently in the works would not be implemented until 2012 at the earliest. And any action would still require another five to ten years to take effect, making the earliest possible drop in carbon emissions some time around 2020. By then, the authors fear, shipping emissions could represent up to 6 per cent of global carbon emissions. Bill Hemmings, policy officer with the *independent European Federation for* Transport and Environment (EFT&E) commented, 'The majority has succumbed to the blocking tactics of a small minority. They clearly have not seized the urgency of the issue.' John Maggs of Seas At Risk (an association of NGOs working to protect European seas and the wider North East Atlantic), another group that was involved in the issuing of the statement, added, 'The IMO has reached the point it should have attained five to ten years ago.'[7]

In the wake of the meeting, as Kyoto millstones began to hang around shipping's neck, luminaries in the industry hit back. The International Chamber of Shipping (ICS), for one, dismissed the idea that the Kyoto Protocol concept of 'common but differentiated responsibility' should be applied to shipping. ICS chairman, Spyros M. Polemis, said in a statement:

> The IMO has an impressive track record of adopting standards for shipping that are applied equally. The shipping industry argues that the current Kyoto Protocol concept of 'common but differentiated responsibility' cannot be practically applied to shipping without the danger of significant 'carbon leakage'. Only about 35 per cent of the world merchant fleet is registered in Kyoto Annex I countries which are currently committed to meeting the emissions reduction targets agreed in 1997. We fear that failure in Copenhagen, by the UN Framework Convention on Climate Change (UNFCCC), to agree that IMO should be given a mandate for delivering a CO_2 reduction regime for shipping will greatly reduce the ability of the shipping sector as a whole to reduce its emissions.[8]

According to the ICS, the consensus of opinion within the industry is that it may be possible for ships to reduce CO_2 emitted per tonne kilometre by perhaps 15–20 per cent by 2020 through a combination of technological and operational developments aimed at reducing fuel consumption. In the longer term, advances in alternative fuel technologies may deliver further improvements. These estimates do not, however, take into account claims made for CO_2-scrubbing technology developed by Singapore firm Ecospec, detailed later in the chapter. Fuel switching can reduce about 44 per cent of sulphur dioxide (SO2) emissions, and is the primary approach adopted by MARPOL Annex VI.

ICS said in its statement:

> Shipping is already the most carbon efficient mode of commercial transport, about 30 times more efficient than air freight. But it is fully recognised that CO_2 emissions from the industry as a whole – some 3 per cent of all global emissions – are comparable to those of a major national economy. The shipping industry accepts that the CO_2 emissions reduction which ships must aim to achieve should be at least as ambitious

151

as the emissions reduction agreed under any new United Nations Climate Change Convention.[9]

Despite all this soul searching, the industry turned up in droves to chilly Copenhagen in December 2009 with no consensus on how best to emit less. There was vocal support by leading shipping bodies to ensure the IMO will be the enforcer of any new green regulations. Beyond that, however, agreements were few and far between.

The European Union, several African nations, Norway, Mexico and Australia proposed an international cap-and-trade system covering ships and airlines that could raise as much as US$25 bn a year. That money could then be used to help the poorest nations shift to renewable energy, slow deforestation and adapt to climate change. The EU also pushed for 2020 targets of a 20 per cent cut in maritime emissions to below 2005 levels.

China, India, Saudi Arabia and the Bahamas strongly opposed controls on their shipping and aviation, forcing deadlock. 'Negotiators have so far failed to see beyond their own narrow or group interests,' said EFT&E 's Bill Hemmings as the clock ticked down to the final hours of the convention. 'They are currently hemmed in by stale political positions.'

For all the huge attention and importance placed on Copenhagen, the whole summit achieved nothing. The travel footprint of the 35,000 attending the summit was estimated by the US media network PBS at being in the region of 110 mn pounds of CO_2. There was a lot of late-night horse-trading, much hot air but little in the way of tangible results. Aviation and shipping are likely to have to face regional curbs in the future.

As Neville Smith presciently wrote in *Lloyd's List* newspaper seven months ahead of Copenhagen:'The argument which has swept back and forth on SOx, NOx and particulate matter has at times been a metaphor for the shipping industry: on one hand innovative, on the other riven by factional disagreements.'[10] Inaction has resulted in regional splinter actions, which in their own way make international trade that much harder.

For instance, vessels sailing off the coast of California now face the world's toughest rules on marine fuel use under new regulations adopted by the State's Air Resources Board that came into effect in 2009. The board maintains its decision will eliminate 15 tonnes of diesel exhaust daily from ocean-going vessels, and will substantially reduce cancer rates and premature deaths associated with living near seaports and trade corridors along California's coast. Effective from 1 July 2009, ocean-going ships must use low-sulphur marine distillates within 27.6 miles of the California coast. The law is a two-step one that will eventually see sulphur content limited to 0.1 per cent by 2012.

In May 2005 the first Sulphur Emission Control Area (SECA) was formed for the Baltic Sea and a more stringent 1.5 per cent cap came into force in this zone. The North Sea and the English Channel became part of the first SECA in 2006. Starting in 2008 SECAs became simply Emission Control Areas (ECA) to allow caps to be introduced for other forms of emissions such as NOx. The EU has now stepped up its sulphur reduction plans to the chagrin of owners and oil corporations alike. It announced in 2009 that from as early as 1 January 2010 all ships at berth in EU waters will have a 0.1 per cent sulphur limit on all marine fuels. The oil companies and INTERTANKO shot back that such swift adoption of the rules would be impossible to achieve. The original deadline had been set for 2015. Until there is uniform global regulation, the owners and oil majors maintained, ships will effectively have to carry three grades of fuel onboard and may not have the segregated tanks to do so. In addition, switching from heavy fuel oil to marine gasoil carries inherent safety risks relating to furnace explosions. The industry requires greater time to implement modifications and training, they urged. Moreover, question marks remain over the availability of sufficient supplies of 0.1 per cent sulphur content fuel.

It is the EU that gives ship owners the greatest headache, and not just with the ECAs. The EU is likely to push ahead with a carbon credit system within four years. Shipping may drive up demand for carbon credits by as much as 15 per cent if it is brought within the European Union cap-and-trade scheme, according to climate change specialist Anne-Marie Warris from the British classification society Lloyd's Register.[11] The anticipated bill for the shipping industry at current carbon prices is €4 bn ($6 bn) a year, starting from 2013, she noted.

Ships carrying commodities and containers globally release about 870 mn tonnes of CO_2 equivalent, equal to that emitted by Europe's leading economy Germany as a whole, Dr Warris said, speaking at a conference in Singapore in October 2009. She was citing 2007 data by the International Maritime Organization. 'SECAs', Bowring in Hong Kong has pointed out, 'are done by western nations, which suits them as they have migrated their manufacturing here to the Pearl River Delta.'[12] And yet the paradox is that shipping is environmentally friendly. No other form of transport gets close to shifting goods so economically and with as little damage to the environment. For instance, a plane emits thirty-six times more CO_2 per kilo per kilometre, while a truck emits three times as much CO_2 (see tables 8.1 and 8.2 above).

'Shipping is environmentally friendly' and is 'an answer to the greenhouse problem, not the problem', says Bowring. Moreover, he has stressed that 'Sea transport is a necessity while air transport is a luxury.'[13] The shipping industry is responsible for the carriage of about 90 per cent of world trade. 'Without shipping, half the world would starve, half would freeze and the rest would both starve and freeze,' states the International Chamber of Shipping.[14] Both the HKSOA and INTERTANKO are pushing for a 1 per cent global cap in sulphur on distillate, not the far heavier fuel oil.

The refiners, who have long enjoyed offloading their otherwise useless fuel to the shipping industry, have objected. Their argument is that they are unable to produce an additional 250 mn tonnes of distillate in the timeframe envisaged and they wonder what they would do with all the residual fuel. HKSOA and INTERTANKO's argument is that clean fuel would largely eliminate the need for purifiers, heating of fuel tanks, sludge control and emission abatement equipment and the disposal of its residues, and would lead to the development of more efficient engines and more sophisticated emission-reduction systems.

One per cent distillate would immediately reduce sulphur dioxide by 60–80 per cent and particulate matter by 80–90 per cent, and since the fuel would not need to be heated onboard that energy could be used to power the ship. A switch to cleaner distillate fuels would assist in the development of more efficient engines, urges Bowring. The switch would not be cheap – fuel costs may rise by as much as US\$200 to US\$250 a tonne, and Bowring, while he represents owners himself, knows them too well to assume they would convert voluntarily. 'We want regulations on this issue. We don't want to leave it to the owner as it is very expensive to switch.'[15]

Solutions: Greenwashing or Not?

Other fuel ideas to make shipping cleaner include switching to biofuels. Getting such huge quantities at the right price and quality is unlikely for many years to come. Others have looked into gas power. The stumbling block here is how to get the fuel supercompressed and stored safely – something the industry has been grappling with for years. In 2008 Singapore's Jenjosh Group successfully debuted a series of fully propelled vessels using compressed natural gas main engines and compressed natural gas generators. 'These are the ships of the future,' said the firm in a widely reported press release to the industry, 'with efficiency in cost and fuel cleanliness – a truly green ship!'[16] However, the vessels, built at a yard in central China, are very small. The world's naval architects continue to rack their brains as to how to supersize this achievement.

Singaporean firm Ecospec has achieved significant results in reducing emissions, including of CO_2 via its scrubber technology. It tested its pioneering technology on a shore-based rig in July 2009, knocking out 55 per cent of the normal CO_2 produced. Another manufacturer of scrubbing technology, UK-based Krystallon, maintains scrubbers can remove 99 per cent of sulphur oxides (SOx) emissions and not just in port but at all times, greatly reducing shipping's contribution of 20 per cent of the world's entire SOx emissions. The other advantage scrubbers have is in the extraction of up to 80 per cent of particulate matter in fuel. However, scrubbing remains an interim, short-term plan to combat emissions.

Certain elements of the industry are wildly innovative and this decade has seen some truly significant green design breakthroughs that give optimism to those who believe firmly that shipping can still self-regulate. The impetus for the rise in all things sustainable was in no small part caused by the spikes in oil prices in recent years which have harmed profits.

Fig. 8.2 SkySails kite-propelled tanker

Among the more revolutionary design teams is Greenwave – a three-year-old charity focused on significantly lowering CO_2 and other emissions by reducing the consumption of fossil fuels. The brainchild of Greek ship manager Costas Apodiacos, the organisation came across an obscure moment in naval design that occurred close to a hundred years ago. Two Germans, one a physicist and the other an engineer, had harnessed the power of the wind in a unique way, using rotors to the same effect as sails. A test ship using this revolutionary technology was successfully ocean-trialled in an Atlantic crossing. Now Greenwave's team have blown the dust off that proven invention and, using modern technology and materials, brought it up to date.

The wind engine uses a phenomenon known as the Magnus effect, which was first discovered by the German chemist and physicist Gustav Magnus in 1852. When wind hits a spinning vertical cylinder it creates a very low pressure on one side that generates lift and hence thrust much like a sail does. The Greenwave Wind Engine generates ten times more propulsion than the equivalent profile area of a sail. Initial wind tunnel tests have indicated that the Greenwave Wind Engines are capable of providing at least 13 per cent of the thrust required to propel a ship, saving 900 tonnes of fuel per year. Greenwave has not stopped there. It has also developed a plastic jacket drag kit that improves a vessel's aerodynamics and can easily be installed.

Greenwave has dismissed the idea of using sails or giant kites to move a cargo vessel, maintaining that the surface area of a sail would need to be at least two and a half thousand square yards to make a significant impact on fuel consumption. However, one German firm has come up with a giant kite system that clearly delivers fuel savings. Hamburg-based SkySails claims that depending on the prevailing wind conditions, it can be used to reduce a ship's average annual fuel costs by 10–35 per cent. Under optimal wind conditions, fuel consumption can temporarily be cut by up to 50 per cent. The system has been trialled successfully to much fanfare in the industry. Its limitations are that at present it cannot shift heavily laden vessels. Designers are working to increase its capabilities.

The Swedish shipping company Stena Bulk showed off its latest environmental ship design, the E-MAXair, at a show in Norway in the summer of 2009. The ship will incorporate SkySails as well as an optimised hull design, and a specially developed and patented hull construction based on an air-pocket system under the vessel. In addition, the tanker is designed for operation with liquefied natural gas. Stena claims the ship will be the most environmentally friendly tanker in the world.

Another renewable is making waves too: the power of the sun. In August 2009 the *Solon* was launched in Berlin, becoming the German capital's first passenger ship that is driven by solar energy alone. The Berlin-based solar company after which the ship is named also supplied the twenty-four solar modules with a capacity of 5.6 kWp; they are fitted to the ship's roof and supply its drive energy. SolarWaterWorld AG, the manufacturer and operator of the Solon, also operates the world's first solar charging station for solar-powered boats in the Köpenick district of Berlin. 'The future belongs to solar mobility, whether on roads, rails or water and Solon is one of the main drivers of this development,' said Thomas Krupke, CEO of SOLON SE, on the occasion of the launch. The C60 solar catamaran can accommodate up to sixty passengers and will sail on Berlin's waterways providing tours of the city and cruise trips. The ship offers a tangible sign that emission-free mobility is also advancing for inland shipping. A prototype of this craft completed its first Atlantic crossing to New York in 2006.

In late 2009 Smoggy Hong Kong harbour took delivery of four solar ferries built by Sydney's Solar Sailor Holdings. Three-quarters of the power is powered by solar and one-quarter is powered by liquid petroleum gas. Robert Dane, CEO at Solar Sailor, likes to compare his 'hybrid marine power' with Toyota's much-hyped Prius car. When comparing his technology to that of diesel-run motors he explains: 'That industry's had a hundred years to develop the technologies and economies of scale. We're coming in and competing against that in five or 10 years with a system that has to be as good or better and the same price or cheaper.'[17] Now Solar Sailor is in talks with China's largest shipping company to install solar panels on the firm's fleet of tankers.

In Japan, meanwhile, one of the acknowledged leaders in green cargo shipping, Nippon Yusen Kaisha (NYK) has pioneered a car carrier fitted with 328 solar panels. The 656-foot, 60,000-tonne *Auriga Leader*, can carry 6,200 cars and was designed with both Toyota and Tokyo Oil. The panels help reduce emissions by about 10 per cent, according to the designers.

Compatriot Japanese firm Mitsui Engineering & Shipbuilding (MES) is rapidly becoming known as a leader in green shipbuilding, developing designs for VLCCs that will emit 30 per cent less emissions than the current crop of giant ships as a result of tweaking hull design and making the ships more aerodynamic. Now, the company has announced it will join Osaka University in researching a hybrid propulsion system that introduces a battery unit into the diesel engine. MES anticipates that in the future there may be demands to reduce ships' emissions by up to 50–80 per cent for which battery assistance will be necessary.

Fuel cell technology, estimated to be up to 50 per cent more efficient than today's diesel engines, could in the near future transform the economics and environmental impact of commercial shipping. A fuel cell converts the chemically stored energy in a fuel directly to electricity through a reaction with oxygen in the air. The process is very similar to what happens in an ordinary battery, but with the important distinction that a fuel cell does not need to be recharged.

The world's first fuel cell powered passenger ship was launched in August 2008 in Hamburg. Zemships is an EU-supported project which has developed and operated a fuel cell powered passenger ship with a hydrogen fuelling station. The fuel cell powered Zemship has a power of up to 600 kW and can accommodate up to a hundred passengers. The only emission from Zemship is water vapour. Naval architects are now working out how to make this breakthrough technology work with large ocean-going ships.

Another seemingly unlikely idea has recently concluded successful sea trials. Rotterdam-based DK Group proposes boring large holes into the hulls of ships. The idea is to shoot compressed air through the cavities. The airflow from the trial vessel created a buffer of bubbles to reduce drag and, crucially, cut fuel consumption by 10 per cent.

In South Korea, the world's leading shipbuilding nation, the yards are working closely with engine manufacturers to tweak designs to make their products greener. Improved propulsion, through innovations such as adding a fin to a propeller, sleeker hull designs and even different paint, all help save on fuel.

Mohammad Souri, the chairman of the National Iranian Tanker Company (NITC), a shipping giant whose order book puts it on course to become the third largest tanker owner in the world by 2011, is a champion of green tanker design. He has observed that 1 litre of fuel on a modern VLCC moves 1 tonne of cargo more than 1,100 miles. This is more than twice as far as was possible twenty years ago. He outlined some of the measures his firm has taken to help reduce fuel consumption while speaking at a seminar in Singapore in September 2008.

Applying silicon antifouling paint to reduce hull resistance as the ship cuts through the water has reduced his fleet's fuel consumption by 2.1 per cent. Modifying the propeller edge and installing a cap fin propeller brings a 6 per cent saving, while regular underwater hull cleaning helps reduce resistance too. These measures are being taken up by many of the forward-thinking owners around the world, aware that the initial costs will be clawed back quickly with rising bunker prices. But according to Souri the whole industry needs to react as one. 'The costs of delaying action will be far more if we don't act now.' He maintains that CO_2 ship indexing, 'will play an important role in the future'.

Norway is a bit of a pacesetter in green maritime matters, ahead of the curve. The government introduced a NOx tax on shipping firms entering Norwegian waters back in 2007. In May 2008 companies were invited to join and pay into the NOx Fund – more than five hundred have done so far – in exchange for paying less NOx tax. Grants are also handed out to assist in emission-reducing technology. Under the 2002 Gothenburg Protocol, Norway has committed to cut NOx emissions by 30,000 tonnes by 2011. The fund is helping create the technology to smash that target.

One incredible Norwegian vision of the future of waterborne transport has made headlines around the world. The *E/S Orcelle*, named after an endangered Irawaddy dolphin, is a concept ship designed by Wallenius Wilhelmsen, a well-known Norwegian owner. The ship does not release any emissions into the atmosphere or into the ocean. She uses the sun, wind and waves as well as fuel cells to generate the energy required to power the vessel. Solar energy is harnessed through photovoltaic panels in the ship's three sails, which also help propel it using wind power. Wave power is utilised through a series of twelve fins, which will be able to transform wave energy into hydrogen, electricity or mechanical energy. Around half the energy on the *E/S Orcelle* will be produced by fuel cells. By using lightweight materials such as aluminium the ship could carry 50 per cent more than today's car carriers – while having a similar weight in tonnage terms.

There are countless more examples of shipping's innovative side. It is regulatory indecision that is hampering progress.

Ships to the Rescue

Ironically, despite all the negative press shipping has had on its environmental track record of late, the industry could have the answer to combating the whole greenhouse gas issue. Rather than sending rockets into the atmosphere to launch millions of mirrors to deflect the sun's rays, an astronomically expensive idea that had been doing the rounds for a couple of years, in the summer of 2009 a cheaper nautical solution made headlines.

Box 8.1   Relocating the Sea: Ballast Water

Cargo ships, including oil tankers, are designed to carry heavy loads. When not fully laden they take on seawater, known as ballast water, to balance the ship. This water is then discharged at the next port of loading, which may be hundreds or thousands of miles away. Ballast water discharge typically contains a variety of biological materials, including plants, animals, bacteria and viruses. These materials often include non-native, nuisance, exotic species that can cause extensive ecological and economic damage to aquatic ecosystems. For instance, ballast water discharges are believed to be the leading source of invasive species in US marine waters, posing public health and environmental risks, as well as significant economic cost to industries such as water and power utilities, commercial and recreational fisheries, agriculture and tourism. Studies suggest that the economic cost purely from the introduction of pest molluscs (zebra mussels, the Asian clam and others) to US aquatic ecosystems is more than US$6 bn per year.

The IMO introduced a ballast water convention more than five years ago to halt the further spread of invasive species around the world's oceans, but lethargic member states have once again failed to endorse it ringingly. Under the timeline set when the convention was adopted in 2004, it will enter into force twelve months after ratification by thirty states, representing 35 per cent of world merchant shipping tonnage. But IMO figures up to 31 May 2009 show that just eighteen nations, representing 15.3 per cent of global tonnage, have actually ratified the convention. This inaction is leading to regional rules on ballast water quality emerging, just like the ECAs relating to maritime air pollution. A Filipino chief officer of the Greek ship *Theotokos* became the first individual to be convicted under a US law designed to combat the introduction of invasive species into national waters in July 2009.

There are now more than thirty different types of ballast water management systems available to ship owners. Some of the focus has been on chemical treatment of ballast water while other systems have concentrated on electrolysis in the treatment process. All the contraptions await IMO approval, however, which is keeping owners from making expensive decisions on selecting systems for their new ships.

Box 8.2 Where Tankers Go to Die

Members of the IMO adopted the world's first ship recycling convention at the end of a five-day diplomatic conference of the United Nations unit in Hong Kong in May 2009. While this was being hailed as 'a new chapter in IMO's history' by the body's Secretary-General Efthimios Mitropoulos protesters outside condemned the deal as a step backwards.

It provides guidelines for the design, construction, operation and preparation of ships for recycling; the operation of ship recycling facilities in terms of safety and environment; and the establishment of an appropriate implementation mechanism including surveys and certification, inspections and reporting requirements. Also under the new convention there is the need to have an updated inventory of hazardous materials on board a ship.

Two dozen gong-beating protesters, clad in white, from the NGO Platform on Shipbreaking, carried a banner outside the event reading 'Danger IMO Legalizing Shipbreaking Beaches of Death', and the symbolic corpse of a ship recycling worker. The protesters are calling for a ban on ship beaching before recycling. Group director Ingvild Jenssen said the convention would not prevent a single toxic ship from being dumped on the beaches of India, Bangladesh, Pakistan or any other developing nation.

Speaking to delegates after the convention was adopted, Greenpeace representative Rizwana Hasan said: 'When the workers and the environment of developing countries desperately needed a life ring, the IMO threw them useless paper.' Ms Hasan, who is also a member of the Bangladesh Environmental Lawyers Association, said the convention failed to uphold the principles of the Basel Convention on the Control of Transboundary Movements of Hazardous Wastes and their Disposal. The IMO convention permitted companies to export toxic end-of-life ships to developing countries without first pre-cleaning them of toxic materials.

She added that the convention also legitimised the beaching of vessels and rejected funding mechanisms, such as a mandatory ship owners' fund, that could support use of safer and cleaner operations. Beaching of ships is a process whereby vessels are sent full steam ahead and rammed onto the coastline where, piranha-like, workers set about disassembling these old tubs.

Greenpeace and Friends of the Earth both warned that the lack of a ban on beaching 'may turn back the clock by establishing a regime with lower levels of control and standards of performance than those that exist already under the International Labour Organization and Basel convention's legal regimes and guidelines'. Ghana was the only IMO member state that supported a ban on beaching.

Deaths across south Asian ship-breaking yards continue to soar, with more than twenty in Bangladesh alone in the first nine months of the year.

Fig. 8.3 Shipbreaking yard (Alang, India)

Box 8.3   Nuclear Adherent

By his own standards it had been a slightly subdued speech from the normally ebullient president and CEO of the world's largest shipping conglomerate. Speaking at the conference alongside Asia's biggest shipping exhibition in Shanghai in December 2009, Capt Wei Jiafu from China Ocean Shipping Co. (COSCO) left it till the questions and answers session before he dropped the bombshell.

He was at the lectern, just four days before the Copenhagen climate talks were due to begin, talking about slowing down the speed of his container ships as both an economic and a green measure. He then veered off-message. Heads were raised and a light murmuring emanated around the room as he launched into his nuclear power aims. Wei said he was in favour of using nuclear power on board merchant ships as a further green initiative. 'As they are already onboard submarines, why not cargo ships?' he mused. 'If we could prove we are able to use nuclear energy on ships safely this could be one of the solutions.' Later he revealed that COSCO is in talks with the national nuclear authorities to develop nuclear powered ships.

Nuclear power on board ships is nothing new. The US Navy, where commercial considerations are not a hindrance, started developing the concept back in the 1940s. While navies around the world built up a nuclear armada, the history of merchant ships adopting the radioactive technology has thus far been inglorious, largely down to price. The US-built NS *Savannah* was commissioned in 1962 and decommissioned just eight years later, deemed economically unviable. Likewise the German-built *Otto Hahn* was converted to diesel in 1982, ten years after it was built. The Japanese tried and failed. The only success has been in the far north of Russia, where a fleet of ice breakers has proved this technology can work commercially.

At the height of the recent oil peak, just before the global financial crisis broke in autumn 2008, a slew of design houses trumpeted the possibilities of nuclear propulsion as a means to cut operating costs. No emissions, longer service lives, and much faster transit times were touted as big bonuses. A nuclear newbuild would cost six times the price of a conventional new ship – at up to US$900 mn a piece, according to a 2008 American study. Such is the renewed interest in the technology that British classification society Lloyd's Register has been dusting off its nuclear propulsion manuals of the 1960s and 1970s and updating them. 'The technology is there to commence building nuclear ships. The issues regarding their acceptability and the need for a cultural step-change in shipping still need to be addressed so that society is comfortable any risk is being managed,' commented John Carlton, Global Head, Marine Technology & Investigations, Lloyd's Register.

A wind-powered fleet of 1,900 ships would criss-cross the oceans, sucking up seawater and spraying it from the top of tall funnels to create vast white clouds. These clouds would reflect a tiny proportion, between 1–2 per cent, of the sunlight that would otherwise warm the ocean. This would be enough to cancel out the greenhouse effect caused by carbon dioxide emissions. The ships would be unmanned and directed by satellite to locations with the best conditions for increasing cloud cover. They would mainly operate in the Pacific, far enough from land to avoid interfering with rainfall.

A study commissioned by the Copenhagen Consensus Centre, a think-tank that advises governments on how to spend aid money, found that the fleet would cost US$9 bn to test and launch within twenty-five years. This is a fraction of the US$250 bn that the world's leading nations are considering spending each year to cut CO_2 emissions. 'The space sunshade is really just science fiction but cloud whitening ships deserve serious scrutiny,' says Bjorn Lomborg, director of the think-tank.[18]

Shipping in one form or another could still be the solution to the earth's woes.

CHAPTER NINE

The Politics of Pipelines

22 April 2006 – Xishuangbanna, Yunnan Province, China

Like the ancient Romans, the Chinese like to build things straight. Regardless of the impediments ahead there is nothing a Chinese engineer likes better than the prospect of a ravine, mountain or gushing river to counter in the ongoing construction and transformation of modern China. 'Through rather than around' is the mantra for all things transport in China.

There are few places better to observe this in action than in the humid jungles in the south-west of the country. First-time visitors could be forgiven for thinking they had mistakenly traipsed over into Thailand when touring through China's region of Xishuangbanna. Located on the fringes of the Middle Kingdom, bordering Burma and Laos, this stunningly wild land is where China morphs into South East Asia, where many different cultures live side by side, the diktats from Beijing Party Centre seem like a million miles away and local officials roll their eyes at us when we ask them how they are implementing decisions made up north in the capital. Yunnan has more flora species than all of Western Europe and 60 per cent of China's total. It is a very special place.

Xishuangbanna gets its name from the Thai Sip Sawng Panna, which translates as Twelve Rice-Growing Districts. The countryside, full of jungles, hills and ethnic minority communities, is nothing short of spellbinding and the people, which include Dai, Hani, Bulong, Yao, Jinuop and Lahu ethnic minorities, are among the most welcoming in all of China. Adventurous backpackers come here; some might be lucky enough to see the last few remaining wild elephants left in China.

167

Ethnologists hang out here, soaking up the wildly diverse peoples and cultures. It is such a wild, overgrown area with so few people that flora and fauna discoveries continue to be made. In the late 1980s a whole new tribe who spoke an unintelligible language were discovered in the far south-west corner 16 miles from the Burmese border.

This natural wonder in the corner of a densely packed China is something to behold. Yet it is changing and we're being driven at a hellishly fast speed along one of those rapid changes. The engineers who dismiss natural obstacles as part of their daily lives have managed to hack a straight road through the densely packed jungle to Laos, an incredible feat of blood, sweat ... and environmental degradation. And we're moving along it at 90 mph. We finally reach the point where the road runs out and the countryside ahead of us is preparing for its next attack of the diggers.

A straight line has been drawn through the area to the Burmese border and down to the coast. On this line will reside a shiny round steel tube, 7 feet or so wide, stretching for thousands of miles through thick green vegetation, over hills and along paddy fields. Once finished, this pipeline, like the one that bisects the Gobi Desert in the north-west of the country, will profoundly change the energy dynamics of China. The noose of the Malacca Straits will be further loosened. Alternative supply lines – steel cutting through the jungle like a machete – will ease energy planning in Beijing. As if sucking on two giant straws, China's constantly expanding cities will slurp up ever more oil from Burma and Central Asia. We're standing at the end of a road facing jungle. By the time this book is published that jungle will be gone and the road will head on into the distance – straight as an arrow as far as the eye can see.

Pipelines: An Alternative Way to Achieve Energy Security?

Oil pipelines provide a similar benefit to both producers and consumers of oil. They offer a method of delivery that diversifies supplies away from seaborne transportation and the worrisome reliance on a mode of delivery that, as has been shown, can be disrupted by any number of factors. At some point all of the world's oil goes through some sort of pipeline. It may be several thousand miles long and run across vast expanses of largely uninhabited land in Central Asia or lead overland from a port in a fast-growing Chinese industrial city such as Tianjin to supply the 17 mn people in Beijing who daily own more cars, switch on more appliances and demand an uninterrupted supply of energy. In the summer of 2009 Beijingers were buying more cars per month than the whole of the US combined. Pipes can also be relatively short: oil moves from fields of extraction to waiting tankers in ports in the Middle East and Africa by pipe and then from port of arrival to refiner and end user. Without pipelines, short or long, the oil industry would still, literally, be rolling barrels down gangplanks.

Given that, at some point in its transit, approximately 40 per cent of the world's oil flows through a pipeline of significant length they are both vital to the global oil transportation system and one of its fundamental Achilles heels in any number of ways from cost and construction to security and reliability. For instance, Saudi Arabia alone has approximately 2,800 miles of pipeline; Iraq 4,000 miles, much of it above ground and vulnerable to attack. It only takes a simple explosive device to puncture a pipeline and render it non-operational – in 2004 alone saboteurs attacked Iraq's national pipeline system no fewer than a hundred times. In recent years there have been numerous attacks on pipelines in Nigeria, Colombia and Pakistan as well as Iraq, while there have been rumours of attacks on pipelines running through China's Xinjiang province (strenuously denied by Beijing). In July 2009 Nigeria's most prominent militant group, the Movement for the Emancipation of the Niger Delta (MEND), claimed to have sabotaged oil pipelines forcing Anglo-Dutch Shell, Italy's Azienda Generale Italiana Petroli (Agip) and the US oil firm Chevron to cut output by about 273,000 bpd. It has also been reported that a terrorist attack was planned and then thwarted on the crucial Ras Tanura to Riyadh pipeline in central Saudi Arabia, the biggest oil-loading point of the world's biggest oil exporter. If a successful attack had occurred this would have caused havoc with the oil supplies of many nations.

Table 9.1 **Major pipeline countries, 2009**

Country	Length of oil pipeline (km)
USA*	244,620
Russia	72,347
Canada	23,564
China	17,240
Kazakhstan	10,376
Mexico	8,688
Iran	8,438
India	7,883
Venezuela	7,607
Indonesia	7,471
Libya	6,956
Algeria	6,878
Colombia	6,140
Argentina	5,607
Egypt	5,518
Iraq	5,509
Brazil	5,214
UK	4,930
Saudi Arabia	4,521
Ukraine	4,514
Nigeria	4,347
Sudan	4,070
Turkey	3,636
Oman	3,558
Germany	3,546
France	3,032
UAE	2,950
Bolivia	2,475
Norway	2,444
Azerbaijan	2,436
Pakistan	2,076

Source: National statistics
Note: * = all oil products

It is not only in unstable states such as Iraq and Nigeria that pipelines are vulnerable. In recent years the 800-mile Trans-Alaska Pipeline System (TAPS) from Prudhoe Bay to the terminal at Valdez, the sole method of oil delivery from Alaska, has been sabotaged repeatedly, bombed several times and shot at more than fifty times. TAPS has long been controversial. It was built as a response to the 1973 Oil Crisis. Environmental, legal and political debates and challenges have been constant since the discovery of oil at Prudhoe Bay in the 1960s.

Pipelines fall prey to terrorism and disruption to a greater extent than the sea lanes: they are the target of environmental, native peoples and conservationist groups in a way that have not affected seaborne transportation to date. Striking at pipelines achieves two goals: undermining the internal stability of the regime to which the attackers are opposed, and economically weakening foreign powers with vested interests in their region. Given that oil pipelines are usually long by default and often cross remote terrain, they are considered 'soft' targets and hard to defend.

It should also be remembered that oil pipelines are not a cheap option of delivery. For instance, the 1,100-mile Baku–Tbilisi–Ceyhan crude oil pipeline from the Azeri-Chirag-Guneshli field in the Caspian to the Mediterranean coast cost US$3.9 bn to build,[1] while Russia announced in 2007 that it would cost at least US$11 bn to build the first leg of its major oil pipeline to Asia.[2] Estimates of the cost of the entire pipeline's construction range from US$20 bn (at 2006 prices) upwards. This would make the Russia–Asia pipeline extremely expensive at approximately US$3.9–4.0 mn per km of pipeline compared to the British Petroleum (BP)-led Baku-Ceyhan pipe's cost of around US$2.2 mn per km and the Chevron-led CPC pipeline from Kazakhstan to Russia's Black Sea port at Novorossiysk at an apparent bargain price of just US$1.7 mn per km. In recent years pipeline costs have risen dramatically and threatened financing arrangements and completion dates. And these cost overruns and price rises are not insignificant. In 2008 it was announced that the East Siberia-Pacific Ocean oil pipeline was threatened with severe delays and cost overruns. Trasneft, the Russian oil pipeline monopoly, was forced to delay completion of the 1,700-mile first phase linking

Taishet, an oil hub in eastern Siberia, to Skovorodino, a rail hub on the Chinese border, after the project cost soared from the initial estimates of US$6 bn to US$12 bn, i.e. doubled. At the same time repair costs to pipelines are high due to the distances involved, danger to repair crews and weather – for instance, it is impossible to repair the Alaskan TAPS pipeline in the winter.

Whatever the cost, pipelines have long suffered the same problems as any form of land-based transport. They are subject to interruption and disruption, political change and upheaval, attack by dedicated terrorists or disgruntled local communities, technical problems miles from nowhere and erratic weather. At the same time they are inflexible – they cannot suddenly change route to avoid problems in the way tankers can.

Ownership and control of pipelines are issues too, as they are for any transnational phenomena. Who owns the pipe? Who controls the flow? Whose finger is on the off switch? All questions that bedevil 'pipeline politics' and particularly worry nations concerned with ensuring uninterrupted flows of energy. To see how serious nation-states take this issue of interrupted pipeline supplies it is only necessary to look at the concerns of Germany and other EU nations over the Russia–Ukraine pipeline disputes between the Russian state-controlled gas supplier Gazprom and the Ukrainian national oil and gas company Naftohaz Ukrainy over natural gas supplies, prices and debts. The dispute has escalated and threatened natural gas supplies in several European countries that depend on Russian natural gas. Approximately 25 per cent of the EU's natural gas consumption (closer to 40 per cent in Germany) is from Russia and 80 per cent of that is piped through the Ukraine. In July 2009, commenting on the continued problems surrounding the gas pipeline disputes between Russia and Western Europe, the *Economist* stated that, 'He who pays for the pipelines calls the tune', but this is only partly right.[3] Global pipeline politics has traditionally been fraught and required large-scale economic and diplomatic dedication. Yet states with high oil import dependency ratios still need these alternative modes of supply. Again, China is a prime case in point.

The Silk Pipeline

The primary historic trading route between East Asia and the Middle East was of course the Silk Road – the land bridge between the two regions. It functioned for centuries but was always problematic. Caravans could travel from Xian in China and Damascus in Syria but there were constant disruptions and interruptions to trade and supplies – caravans regularly completely disappeared in the shifting sands of the Taklamakan Desert; bandits, marauders and warlords raided the traders; Mongol hordes severed the traditional routes. Arabs had been going to China for some time; mostly as merchants to Guangzhou from the time of the Tang Dynasty (AD 618–907), first reaching China via the Silk Road some time in the seventh century. Accounts of these early Arab visitors to China had started circulating throughout the Muslim world by AD 850 with some accounts recording an Islamic population (which probably included many people from Persia and India too) of about 10,000 by the end of the first millennium, others talk of 120,000 foreigners in Guangzhou alone and 25,000 in the Tang Dynasty's capital city of Chang'an.

By the 1600s the disruption of the land routes into China was such that they were essentially closed down due to war, banditry and political turmoil. The Silk Road died but the sea lanes between the Middle East and the Far East prospered (war, weather and pirates permitting). Trade between the two regions became waterborne and eventually the Europeans also joined that eastward trade. China's media still regularly talk of a new Silk Road (*si chou zhi lu*), but in a country with a long historical memory and a keen sense of sovereignty Beijing remains worried about recurring incidents and issues that threaten its land border. From the point of view of the Chinese leadership, the Sino–Soviet Split of the 1950s resulted in border clashes in the region and further disruptions and cessations of overland trade routes. It does not help, of course, that China's two major land borders towards the west are the internally problematic regions of Xinjiang and Tibet. Yet China's oil dependency and Central Asia's ability to supply is of such importance that keeping those cross-border points open is now deemed absolutely essential.

East Asia is hardly alone in worrying about the fragility of pipeline energy supplies. Europe's energy security and pipeline politics have switched between tragedy and farce as Western Europeans rely on Russian controlled East–West pipelines and worry nervously when they see argument between Moscow and Kiev and supplies being cut off. Russia clearly has the muscle in this relationship. Other countries too have become powerbrokers through pipeline politics: in July 2009 an agreement was signed in the Turkish capital, Ankara, to build a new 2,050-mile gas pipeline called Nabucco to run between eastern Turkey and Vienna. Nabucco involves Bulgaria, Romania and Hungary, along with the two terminus states. Washington gave strong support to the Nabucco project primarily because, it is hoped, that once Nabucco is up and running in 2015, Iraq can be one of the nations that reaps large profits by feeding gas into it, thereby easing the financial situation there. Quite simply pipelines are political.

This political aspect to pipelines leaves some oil consumers uncomfortable. As has been shown, if possible, China prefers a strictly business approach to its oil supply deals and works hard to ensure that no politics or conflicts interfere in its overseas business dealings – at least to its way of thinking. Additionally, Beijing is concerned about conflicts in Africa, the Middle East and the threats of piracy in Africa, the Straits of Hormuz and the Malacca Straits. Pipelines potentially offer a solution to all these problems. China looks primarily to Central Asia for a more controllable political situation. Neighbouring Kazakhstan has 3 per cent of world oil supplies and the largest fields are relatively close to the Chinese border – the concept of pipelines from Kazakhstan to China is therefore very appealing to Beijing. They cannot meet all China's oil demand but they can help the country's energy security, Beijing believes.

Consequently, China has begun to pursue pipelines as part of its solution to its growing oil needs, both domestic and transnational, seeking particularly to bolster its energy security by sealing long-term deals with neighbouring Central Asian states (and Russia) to reduce its reliance on maritime oil transportation routes. However, China was not initially successful when it came to ensuring supplies by pipeline. While it has built stronger and closer relationships with the new Central Asian republics of the former USSR through trade, aid, diplomacy and most obviously the Shanghai Five organisation, relations with Russia over pipelines remain strained.

The Shanghai Five, now formally the Shanghai Co-operation Organization (SCO), is an intergovernmental mutual-security grouping founded in 2001 by the leaders of China, Kazakhstan, Kyrgyzstan, Russia, Tajikistan and Uzbekistan. Except for Uzbekistan, the other countries had been members of the Shanghai Five, founded in 1996; after the inclusion of Uzbekistan in 2001. Technically the group was formed after the signing of the *Treaty on Deepening Military Trust in Border Regions* in April 1996, and security-related concerns remain paramount. However, for China the main security-related issue is energy security rather than any threat of invasion or internal turmoil. Aside from the constant members there are any number of important countries that maintain observer status with the SCO – India, Iran, Mongolia and Pakistan, while Sri Lanka and Belarus have been granted dialogue partner status and Afghanistan is currently part of the SCO-Afghanistan Contact Group.

However, tensions over pipelines between Russia and China have been fraught. Russia has both large oil (and gas) reserves as well as a substantial Far Eastern territory stretching across the top of Mongolia through Siberia and down to Vladivostok and the North Korean border. Additionally, there is the issue of competition with Japan, a country with even fewer domestic oil resources than China, an even higher rate of oil-import dependency and a nation with which China has ongoing simmering long-running tensions that have led to various diplomatic flare-ups and protests in recent years. Relations with Taiwan are similar: tensions between Beijing and Taipei remain fraught, with frequent recurrences of sabre rattling between the island and the mainland despite some easing of cross-Straits travel and investment restrictions in recent years. Taiwan has no domestic oil reserves and is unable feasibly to connect to any pipeline unless it comes from the Mainland. Taiwan is therefore forced to rely on seaborne oil supplies.

China's major overland solution is the Kazakhstan–China oil pipeline, China's first direct oil import pipeline allowing oil to flow from Central Asia. It also happens that this pipeline is a good example of the complex web of national, regional and business interests that invariably bedevil pipelines. Running from Kazakhstan's Caspian shore to Xinjiang (officially the Xinjiang Uygur Autonomous Region), the pipeline is jointly owned by the state-owned China National Petroleum Corporation (CNPC) and the state-owned Kazakh oil company KazMunaiGaz. The construction of the pipeline was agreed between China and Kazakhstan in 1997 and the final Kenkiyak–Kumkol section between Kazakhstan and China was completed in July 2009. The 1,384-mile pipeline has a capacity of 120,000 bpd, though, according to CNPC, that capacity could be upped to 180,000 bpd in the future. Oil in the pipeline comes from more than one source – the main supply source is Kazakhstan's Kashagan field but the pipeline is also used to transport oil from Russia's western Siberia via a connection with the (rather long-windedly named) Russo–Kazak–Turkmenistan–Omsk–Pavlodar–Shymkent pipeline. Two Russian companies transport this oil: TNK-BP (50 per cent owned by BP and 50 per cent by a group of prominent Russian investors known as AAR) and Gazprom Neft (part state, part private but all Russian). Consequently, supplies through the pipeline rely on at least four companies, four countries and a mix of state and private interests cooperating and remaining stable and at peace. And this is far from certain with Kazakhstan in a regional conflict with Uzbekistan, a simmering Turkmenistan–Azerbaijani dispute, continually fractious internal Russian politics, a distinctly colder climate in Moscow towards foreign oil and gas firms' involvement in Russia's energy sector and the outbreaks of unrest in China's Xinjiang region in the summer of 2009. At the same time Azerbaijan, Kazakhstan and Turkmenistan are landlocked and rely wholly on pipelines to ship their oil (with the exception of some shipments across the Caspian Sea to Russia and Iran, who do not need oil anyway). China is hoping to secure further control over the pipe through ongoing talks (that have stalled as of writing) between CNPC and KazMunaiGaz for the Chinese oil company to purchase a 49 per cent stake in Kazakhstan's fourth largest oil producer.

Given the interconnected web of interests, solving issues around pipelines threatens to get messy – each country through which a pipeline passes can demand transit fees and can therefore, theoretically, switch off the flow for any reason, financial, political or economic. As noted in previous chapters, China feels able to become involved in multilateral anti-piracy efforts as this does not position the PRC against any particular nation state or even political group but rather against seemingly rogue elements everyone agrees need controlling and suppressing. However, intervention to protect pipelines, or even further to secure oil wells, is still unthinkable in Beijing in terms of its foreign policy – non-intervention remains the mainstay of China's foreign policy even concerning issues closer to home, such as North.Korean nuclear weapons, the Burmese junta or elsewhere. China, of course a UN Security Council member, tends to abstain whenever intervention or even sanctions are muted against countries – even countries it has historically not been that close to, such as Israel. Moving troops in, even independently or potentially as part of a multilateral force under regional, Shanghai Five (the group's provisions do allow for it) or UN control has so far not happened or even been seriously considered. But China's oil import dependency is growing and so its foreign policies and rationales may have to change too.

Clearly China has felt the need not to be reliant solely on seaborne oil supplies while its own internal priority of developing the inland regions, such as the 'Go West' initiative or the general encouragement of manufacturers and factories to establish themselves inland, requires greater energy delivery to the western portions of the country as opposed to the traditional manufacturing boom areas of southern China (Guangdong province) and the eastern seaboard. Since the end of the Cold War China has increasingly viewed Central Asia through the prism of its western development strategy. It is the case that Central Asia is home to a number of extremist or terrorist organisations that operate in Uzbekistan, Kazakhstan, Kyrgyzstan and Tajikistan (not to mention the occasional accusations from Beijing that 'splittists' operating in Xinjiang have been financed, trained and sheltered in one or other Central Asian nation), although the threat level varies according to the country and region. It is clear that some of these groups are concerned about Beijing's actions in Xinjiang against the Muslim Uyghur population and may seek to take action against China.

Xinjiang is a domestic trouble spot for Beijing. However, the country's drive to secure its energy supplies by pipeline means that Xinjiang is important because all Central Asian pipelines transit the region. China imported in excess of 4.98 mn tonnes of crude oil through the China–Kazakh oil pipeline in 2008, an increase of 24 per cent over 2007.

Box 9.1 China's Growing Pipeline Network

Start point	End point	Details
Domestic:		
Dagang	Beijing	Tianjin port supplying Beijing
Dagang	Nanjing	Tianjin port supplying the capital of Jiangsu province in eastern China
Daqing	Dandong	major Chinese oil production centre running to the North Korean border
Lenghu	Lanzhou	oil-producing centre in Qinghai province supplying neighbouring Gansu province
Maoming	Zhanjiang	connecting central to coastal Guangdong province
Qianjiang	Nanyang	connecting the Nanyang oil field with the municipality of Chongqing (population approximately 31 mn)
Shengli	Qingdao	connecting the Shengli oil field with the port of Qingdao
Shengli	Luoyang	connecting the Shengli oil field with Henan province
Shenyang	Dalian	connecting north-east industrial city with northern port of Dalian
Urumqi	Karamay	connecting the Karamay oil field in western China with the Xinjiang capital of Urumqi
Yanchang	Xian	connecting the Yanchang oil field in eastern China with the city of Xian in Shaanxi province
Zhongyuan	Keifeng	from Zhongyuan oil fields to Kaifeng in Henan province

Chongqing	Nanjing	Zhong-Wu Gas Transportation Pipeline connecting Chongqing Municipality to the city of Nanjing
Jingbian	Shanghai	WestEast Pipeline Phase I connecting to Shanghai
Maoming	Dalian	Chinese LNG Gas Grid following coast with spurs to LNG import terminals
Yacheng	Sanya	supply from Mainland China to Hainan Island
Yacheng	Hong Kong	supply from Mainland China to Hong Kong
Urumqi	Jingbian	West-East Pipeline Phase II between Xinjiang and Shaanxi province
Zhongba	Chongqing	From the Zhongba oil and gas field in Sichuan province to Chongqing Municipality
Kunming	Maoming	delivered sea borne supplies from Guangdong to Sichuan
Chongqing	Lanzhou	connecting Lanzhou oil refinery to Chongqing Municipality
Mangya	Lhasa	connecting remote Qinghai refinery with Tibet

Cross-border:

Shwe field	Kunming	Burma to Sichuan province
Aktyubinsk	Xinjiang	Kazakhstan-China Pipeline to Xinjiang capital
Novokuznetsk	Urumqi	Russia-China Pipeline to Xinjiang capital

Source: Authors' research and China National Energy Administration

Sea-Lane and Pipeline Combos

While nations like China are looking at alternative deliveries from
pipelines to reduce their dependence on seaborne deliveries in the
future, pipelines can also offer alternatives to existing seaborne
problems. There is a pipeline that takes Russian and Central Asian
oil from the Black Sea and runs it through a pipe from the Israeli
port of Ashkelon on the Mediterranean 158 miles to Eilat on the Red
Sea, where it could be loaded onto tankers and shipped to Asia, thus
avoiding the Persian Gulf. The Ashkelon–Eilat pipe was originally
designed to transport crude oil from Iran to Europe but can be used
in reverse to supply India, China and all of East Asia.

Even more ambitious are the highly secretive Sino–Burma pipeline
projects linking Burma's deepwater port of Sittwe (or Kyaukphyu) in
the Bay of Bengal with Kunming in China's Yunnan province. Talks
on the pipe began in 2004 and in 2007 plans to build oil and gas
pipelines from Burma to China were approved by the powerful and
important National Development and Reform Commission (NDRC)
in Beijing. In 2008 Beijing and Burma's military junta agreed to build
a US$1.5 bn oil pipeline (and a US$1.04 bn natural gas pipeline), and
in 2009 a further agreement was reached to build an additional crude
oil pipeline. All the pipes essentially follow the traditional 750-mile
route of the old Burma Road through Lashio and the Shan States to
Kunming (and on to destinations in Yunnan and Guizhou provinces
as well as the heavily populated Chongqing Municipality at the head
of the Yangtze River) with a capacity of up to 22 mn tonnes of crude
oil annually. The aim is to diversify China's crude oil imports routes
from the Middle East and Africa, avoid the pirate and congestion-
prone Malacca Straits and pipe straight into Western China without
the need to berth tankers on China's crowded eastern seaboard and
then pipe to the west internally. Beijing claims the pipeline will prove
to be a cheaper route compared to the existing oil cargo channel
through the Malacca Straits. The cost will be approximately US$2.5
bn and, given Burma's parlous financial state, is to be shouldered
almost entirely by China. Indeed China's state-owned CNPC will
effectively own the pipe with a 50.9 per cent stake and control of the
management of the project, with Myanmar Oil and Gas Enterprise

(MOGE – 100 per cent state-owned) the other partner controlling the remaining 49.1 per cent.

Pipeline politics, even more so than issues around seaborne transportation, reveal the tensions and fragilities of many international relationships. Burma is a current case in point. Neither China nor India has criticised the Rangoon regime over recent political actions including the 2008 street protests by monks, the human tragedy of Cyclone Nargis (where recovery efforts were hampered by seeming junta intransigence) or the continuing house arrest of Aung San Suu Kyi. China and India are too focused on their rivalry for influence in Rangoon, which they both consider their 'backyard', and with the military junta, to access both the country's oil and gas fields and cross-country transportation routes. To this end both nations have been happy to sell arms to Burma, offer large amounts of aid and become involved in infrastructure projects (as have both South Korea and Japan) – China is estimated to be responsible for US$850 mn of the total US$980 mn that was invested in Burma in 2008 and trade between the two countries is worth approximately US$2.6 bn while trade between India and Burma is thought to be worth approximately US$1 bn.[4]

India, with its current 'Look East' policy, fears Burma will fall totally under the control of China; China values access to Burma's resources and Indian Ocean coast. David Mathieson, of Human Rights Watch, has put the situation succinctly, 'In addition to the trade, China is the main political protector of Burma. India, meanwhile, is quite happy to go on being the silent partner.'[5] The situation clearly has the potential to become considerably more tense with the recent pipeline agreements.[6] China, it seems, has won the competition to control the cross-Burma pipelines into its territory while India appears to have the upper hand in developing Burma's Sittwe gas fields and strategic port (which would provide both coastal access and access via India's Kaladan River) on the country's north-west coast.

Chinese involvement in Burma has many in India nervous. As we saw in chapter 4 ('Securing the SLOCs'), India is already worried about Chinese naval vessels in the Indian Ocean and Indian military analysts, seeing China building roads and pipelines from the Burmese coast to south-western China, are increasingly concerned about Chinese longer-term aims in the Indian Ocean. It is the case that Chinese monitoring sites and refuelling capabilities in the Bay of Bengal are extending China's reach into the Indian Ocean but Beijing feels it needs both to conduct longer-range naval missions to protect its oil supplies and commercial shipping from the Horn of Africa, through the Indian Ocean and the Malacca Straits as well as to safeguard its cross-Burma pipelines. These longer-term concerns have already led New Delhi to abandon its one-time policy, held prior to 1993, of attempting to isolate the Burmese regime and trying to involve a host of nations from the Association of South East Asian Nations (ASEAN) to counter what India perceives as a threat from Chinese involvement with Rangoon. These attempts to work more closely with a range of governments from Jakarta to Hanoi and Singapore and Manila on this issue did appear to be yielding fruit for some time. However, the more proactive drive of Chinese soft power across the region from the mid-1990s appears to have largely countered these efforts. It now appears to most observers that Beijing, and not New Delhi, has the upper hand in Burma.

The Burmese example of competing powers seeking influence shows two things: first, that the issue of pipelines is often inseparable from the wider issues surrounding the world's SLOCs and, second, that these twin issues of sea lanes and pipelines can lead to a growth in inter-nation suspicion and rivalry with the possibility of exacerbating tensions. In Central Asia, China may be dealing with a solely land-based issue of pipelines, but in examples like Burma the proposed pipelines come hand-in-hand with the need to secure the SLOCs connecting to them as well. In this case the Chinese desire to pipe oil across Burma to Yunnan, thereby saving costs and the potential congestions and interruptions of the Malacca and Singapore Straits, has meant that China has had to newly prioritise the security of the Bay of Bengal.

Pipe Dreams

Pipelines are impractical for some territories for reasons of geography and distance (in Australia and New Zealand, for instance) and in others due to political problems (Taipei vs Beijing, Seoul vs Pyongyang). Nevertheless, these countries are still working on possible pipeline deals. Taiwan is hoping that the recent easing in cross-Straits tensions that has seen additional direct shipping services and airline routes between the two Chinas as well as increased investment, trade and tourism will lead to the possibility of sub-sea pipelines between the PRC and ROC, though naturally some in Taipei are nervous about reliance on oil supplies from the mainland. South Korea too is exploring sub-sea pipelines that avoid the need to cross DPRK territory – Russia's state-run Gazprom, has entered into talks with the Korea Gas Corporation (KOGAS), the largest LNG importer in the world, about shipping Russian natural gas to South Korea. However, Alexey Miller, chairman of the Management Committee of Gazprom, has stated that an undersea pipeline is problematic and 'not an easy option to take in terms of engineering and cost'.[7] Miller prefers the option of shipping oil and gas to South Korea via VLCCs and gas carriers or an overland pipe through North Korea, the latter being an option that raises more than a few concerns in Seoul.

Despite their drawbacks and vulnerability, oil pipelines are here to stay and there will be more of them from more places to an increasing number of destinations. Countries such as China and Japan will continue to work with oil suppliers and third parties, such as Burma and Russia, to extend pipes and construct new ones. The reliance on imported oil in so many countries effectively guarantees that they will seek to diversify their sources of supply both in terms of where it comes from and how it is transported. At the same time, while ships will continue to deliver the vast bulk of the world's oil supplies from A to B, as long as they remain prone to potential disruption through chokepoints or piracy pipelines and the political risks associated with them they will be deemed necessary evils by consuming nations.

With China's combined strengths of growing diplomatic power and extensive treasury of US$2 trn, along with the thirst for oil, driving their determination, negotiation seems to be paying off in terms of securing piped supplies from Russia and Central Asia. In 2009 the Russian government approved an agreement with Beijing to construct a branch of the Eastern Siberia–Pacific Ocean (ESPO) oil pipeline, providing access to long-term Russian oil supplies with an expected annual throughput of 15 mn tonnes of crude oil. This pipeline would connect Skovorodino in Russia's Amur Oblast to Mohe in China's north-eastern Heilongjiang province, significantly far away from China's more troublesome western region of Xinjiang and so, to Chinese eyes, more secure. Around the same time Beijing agreed a US$700 mn loan between the Export-Import Bank of China and the Russian Bank of Foreign Trade.

Contentious Alternatives

Pipelines are more contentious than shipping with most people and governments but they do provide an alternative to total seaborne oil dependency for many nations. But controversy is never far away and more pipelines will mean more controversies. Sometimes the controversy is environmental – for instance the direct pipeline link between Russia and China through Russia's Altai Republic has attracted campaigners seeking to preserve the Ukok Highlands, the natural habitat of the snow leopard and other endangered species, while the TAPS pipeline in Alaska has been consistently controversial with Alaskan native groups and conservationists. Sometimes the controversies are national: planned and existing pipelines from Siberia, and whether they will route to China or Japan, are perennial subjects of disputes, while China's proposed pipelines through Burma have attracted criticism from opponents of the Rangoon junta and various organisations among the Shan States tribes. Disputes have also arisen over the use of foreign labour to construct pipelines: the China Petroleum Pipeline Engineering Corporation (CPPE) has provided thousands of Chinese workers for pipeline projects in India and Africa, attracting criticism from local community activists. The list of grievances goes on and all could potentially delay the construction, wreck or lead to disruptions in the operation of pipelines countries consider vital to their national interests.

Even so those emerging countries with the highest oil dependency will continue to pursue pipelines and provide funding for pipeline projects that benefit them. Countries that seek to sell their oil on the international market but suffer from bottlenecks in transmission welcome funding of pipelines. All the East Asian countries are involved in new pipeline projects and compete among one another for influence. Among others:

- China's CNPC is considering funding the construction of multiple oil pipeline routes from some land-locked countries in Africa, including Niger and Chad, to the Red Sea ports of Sudan, the Mediterranean and the Gulf of Guinea. These efforts can be seen as critical options for those oil-producing countries in the region, and more importantly, make CNPC a stronger player in Africa.
- Japan's Bank for International Cooperation (JBIC[8]) loaned South Africa's state transport company Transnet US$357 mn in 2009 to fund the widening and deepening of the entrance to Durban Harbour and the construction of a new multi-product pipeline between Durban and Gauteng to replace the existing Durban to Johannesburg pipeline (now more than forty years old) as well as significantly to increase pipeline capacity.
- India recently completed a US$200 mn pipeline to link Port Sudan on the Red Sea with the Sudanese capital Khartoum. At the first India-Africa summit in April 2008, Prime Minister Manmohan Singh said that India's renewed interest in Africa had 'nothing to do with Chinese expansion in the region' telling the media in New Delhi that India was 'not in a race or competition with China or any other country'.[9]

The global competition for oil supplies between the East Asian oil-import dependent countries that we have seen being fought elsewhere around the world is also now being keenly fought wherever new pipelines are being considered or needed.

CONCLUSION

The Future of Moving Oil

Saturday 11 October 2008 – Mailiao Port, Taiwan

The Shinyo Ocean *arrived about 5 miles outside Mailiao Port on Taiwan's heavily industrialised western coast late at night and anchored up before being joined by a local pilot to guide the giant tanker into its dock early the following morning. Mailiao is the largest industrial location for Taiwan's giant conglomerate Formosa Plastics and includes an oil refinery capable of processing 450,000 bpd, a naphtha-cracking plant capable of producing 1.35 mn tonnes of ethylene per year, a 3 GW coal-burning power plant and Taiwan's first wind power plant. The oil refinery was the final destination for the* Shinyo Ocean's *180,000 tonnes of oil. Formosa Plastics needs the oil. Not only is it the largest producer of plastics in Taiwan, but it is also the largest manufacturer of PVC resins in the world and Taiwan's top petrochemical producer.*

It's barely light when the pilot from Mailiao comes aboard and starts the process of slowly guiding the VLCC to its berth. By lunchtime the Shinyo Ocean *is moored up, the paperwork is being processed and the pipes are being attached to the ship's tanks to offload the oil to Formosa Plastics' giant storage tanks. We take our leave of the ship and its crew and head over to the port authorities to complete customs and immigration formalities to enter the Republic of Taiwan. The captain will eventually come ashore for a few hours to arrange for some fresh water and supplies for the* Shinyo Ocean *but the rest of the crew will remain on board until the offloading is completed. Then the* Shinyo Ocean *will leave port, turn around and sail non-stop back to Fujairah to collect another 180,000 tonnes of oil. The cycle continues – the UAE*

187

extracts and exports, the Shinyo Ocean *transports, Formosa Plastics'
refinery refines and the manufacturers of Taiwan manufacture.*

On the 'High Seas'

Everyone has heard the term 'international waters', where the seas
transcend international boundaries and are outside national jurisdiction
– these are the 'high seas'. International waters are both a blessing and
a curse – they allow for the passage of the ships of all nations on the
high seas free of national control, taxes and interference. Yet the high
seas are also where the SLOCs in need of policing travel, where men
and women work in a legal grey area, where piracy and other maritime
crimes often occur and where accidents happen that then impinge on
national coastlines.

International waters and control of the high seas are disputed
concepts in any number of places from the Arctic (Canada, Denmark,
Russia and Norway all regard parts of the Arctic seas as 'national waters'
while the US and most European countries regard the whole region as
international waters) to the numerous small islands in the South China
Seas that occasionally spark disputes and appear in the newspapers.
The Spratly Islands and the Diaoyutai Islands are examples where the
United Nations Convention on the Law of the Sea (UNCLOS) remains
disputed by various nations including China, Japan, South Korea,
Taiwan, the Philippines, Brunei, Malaysia and Vietnam. In many crucial
places the high seas remain zones of intra-national contention.

The modern origins of the freedom of the seas can be traced back to
the South China Sea, the imperative of trade and competing accusations
of piracy. In the early 1600s competition around the Spice Islands of
South East Asia and war at home between the European powers saw
Spain and Portugal accuse the Dutch of piracy and vice versa. Everyone
considered the English to be out-and-out pirates and the Chinese were
alarmed by the presence of all these Europeans in what they considered
to be their waters. The Dutch East India Company (known as the
Vereenigde Nederlandsche Geoctroyeerde Oostindische Compagnie, or
more simply the VOC) wanted to prove that it was not a band of pirates
but acting in its own legitimate commercial interests.

A smart young lawyer from Delft by the name of Grotius gave them their proof in 1608 with an argument entitled *The Spoils of War*. It decried the Spanish naval blockade of Dutch shipping in Asian waters as an act of war. He followed this up with a much more closely argued legal argument entitled *Mare Liberum* or *The Freedom of the Seas*. Grotius voiced the then novel argument that all nations had the right to trade and that no state had the right to prevent nationals of any other state from using the world's sea lanes for the free pursuit of trade. If trade was free, then the seas over which the trade was conducted should also be free.

Grotius's argument (which, to be fair, was a thinly veiled argument for Dutch piracy in the contemporary South China Seas) has basically held ever since. The freedom of the seas was one of American President Woodrow Wilson's Fourteen Points proposed after World War I. Wilson was overly optimistic – Britain and France, both of course massive naval powers, opposed the point. Today, the concept of the freedom of the seas is enshrined in the United Nations Convention on the Law of the Sea under Article 87(1) which states: 'the high seas are open to all states, whether coastal or land-locked'.

International waters free from interference are an essential notion to the free movement of oil around the world by tanker. The protections of that freedom are essential to the global economy. However, guaranteeing the freedom of the high seas is proving harder and harder as they become more crowded with ships of ever more nations moving from an ever greater number of points of departure to ports of arrival.

Preparing for the Future

Let us conclude where we started, with strategic petroleum reserves. Reserves are the crucial backup generators, the spare hard drive of national economies. They ensure that even if war, terrorism, natural disaster or shipwrecks disrupt oil flows for a short period then national economies can keep on functioning – that factories continue to operate, armies to mobilise and that the lights don't go out. As we have seen, most countries in the world, whether they are developed or emerging economies, have substantially lower reserves than the equivalent of ninety days of the prior year's net oil imports – sometimes, as in the case of massively important economies such as China, barely a fortnight's worth. Countries are seeking to build strategic reserves to protect their economies, especially those countries most dependent on oil imports. China is in the process of building eight new state strategic crude oil reserve bases to store additional reserve supplies of oil. It is a serious and expensive undertaking – it is estimated that the first phase of construction alone, to build tanks capable of storing 113 mn cubic feet of crude and 71 mn cubic feet of refined oil, will cost US$1.46 bn.

These tanks are only one component of China's strategy to bolster its energy security. Additionally, annual oil refining volumes will be raised by 18 per cent by 2011 and state petrochemical companies will be encouraged to merge while the government has announced preferential lending rates for oil investments overseas as part of Beijing's November 2008 US$586 bn stimulus package. Oil demand may have dipped temporarily due to the global recession, but China is taking the advantage of the breathing space to prepare itself for a future upturn and to rebound with heightened energy security and improved strategic reserves.

It is not just China that is looking to improve its reserves. In May 2009 the members of ASEAN as well as China, South Korea and Japan (commonly known as ASEAN+3) began drafting an 'oil stockpiling roadmap' as part of a region-wide energy security plan for East Asia. The roadmap, to be established by 2010, will allow individual nations of ASEAN+3 to negotiate bilateral agreements on oil supply security.

Improving strategic reserves will certainly help oil import dependant and industrialising nations such as India, China and all of East Asia to ensure their economic growth. However, improved reserves do not provide enough cover to allow them to ignore the myriad problems of oil transportation by sea detailed in the previous chapters. It is improved relationships with producer nations, ensuring the freedom of the SLOCs and chokepoints of the world's oceans, combating threats such as piracy and promoting the efficient and smooth running of the world oil tanker fleet, that will ultimately ensure uninterrupted flows, meaning that those stockpiled reserves against emergencies remain just that – stockpiles only to be touched when absolutely necessary.

The Scramble for Oil

Corporations are bending over backwards to win contracts, governments are using aid packages as inducements to gain access to oil reserves, diplomats are fawning over regimes they may find distasteful to open doors for their oil corporations, and navies are patrolling the seas to ensure delivery. In a sense, the struggle to gain access to commodities and then ensure their uninterrupted supply is how empires begin – this was true of the British in the nineteenth century and the Americans in the twentieth. Nations need to source and control commodities to fuel their domestic growth, their industry and their military. Historically, over time the need to ensure a constant and uninterrupted flow of commodities has often meant that nations come gradually to extend their power and influence until they end up controlling the territory from which they source the commodities. This, of course, does not have to be in the sense of traditional nineteenth-century European imperialism and colonialism but can take other forms – from aid and investment 'with strings' to engendering vassal states, backing proxies and purchasing the sovereign territory of other nations. We are currently seeing all of these and other strategies at work around the world. They include securing commodities by devoting large sums of money to enhancing energy security (China, in particular, has substantially raised its outbound financial investment in energy: see Table 10.1), the Iraq War, China and India's involvement in Africa and Burma, the creation of a multinational task force around the Horn of Africa, the establishment of organisations such as the Shanghai 5, and continued support for the unelected elites of the oil-producing Middle Eastern states.

The increasing shift in the world's oil flow from West to East and now increasingly from the Middle East (and elsewhere – Africa, Latin America, etc.) to East Asia was initially a phenomenon determined by economics. Both the Asian continent's demographic and territorial giants – India and China – had effectively closed their economies to trade until the 1980s and 1990s. For differing reasons both sought to limit (India) or wholly exclude (China during its Maoist years of attempted self-sufficiency) outside influence. Neither attempt worked – highly controlled economies, central planning and self-sufficiency (even on land masses as large as China's) were found to be unworkable in terms of delivering long-term growth and modern societies. India's economic rise has been slower and less dramatic (and consequently less oil consuming) than China's, which has rapidly boomed and demanded ever-larger supplies of oil. China has a long coastline that supported port facilities where its most successful economic hotspots were located, requiring minimal pipeline facilities. Bringing in oil by sea was natural, as was the case in the rest of East Asia. As all the regional economies grew so they required additional supplies – the seas were the natural transportation and delivery mechanism.

Table 10.1 **China's outbound investment in energy and power internationally, 2003–2009**

Year	US$ bn
2003	0.9
2004	0.8
2005	5.9
2006	9.0
2007	1.6
2008	10.2
2009*	6.2

Source: Thomson Reuters
Note: * = January–May only

China's desire for energy and other commodities has begun to expose the country to conflict despite Beijing's long-held policy of non-interference within the internal affairs of the countries in which it conducts business. However, as China secures oil-supply deals with a greater range of nations globally, this policy has invariably come to involve cooperation with corrupt elites or unpopular governments which may be in a state of conflict with internal forces. This problem has been most obvious so far in Africa. However, there are numerous other sources of potential conflict, not just in Africa, where resentment of China's involvement is growing amongst many segments of the population, but also in the Middle East where Al-Qaeda often speaks of Middle Eastern oil as having been 'stolen'. China could find itself increasingly at odds with one of Al-Qaeda's most persistent grievances: foreign presence and influence within the Middle East. The role of China in the Middle East oil industry combined with continuing unrest in Xinjiang could be a problematic combination transforming the need for oil from an economic to a political issue. Various affiliates of Al-Qaeda were swift to issue threats to Chinese nationals and interests following the summer 2009 riots in Xinjiang.

However, the future supply of oil to these nations, particularly to the new super consumers like China and India, will not simply be determined by economics but also by politics. For China, and the rest of East Asia, to continue to grow economically, prosper and remain stable, reliable supplies of oil by sea are an essential requirement. The region must now be involved in the stability of the Middle East and other supplier regions (from Darfur to Venezuela; Angola to Central Asia) as well as in combating threats to seaborne supply from piracy and other factors that influence the smooth and uninterrupted flow of the SLOCs. The increased flow of oil to East Asia may have started as an economic consequence of the region's rise but its continuance will be a political issue as much as an economic one – and therein lies a host of new challenges for China, the nations of East and South Asia, the rest of the world and the agencies and bodies governing and regulating the seas.

The Future is a Volume Game

As far as this book is concerned, the important thing about the future of the global oil market is not the price – though clearly oil hitting US$100 a barrel or more, as the IEA expects it to (US$120 by 2030 some have predicted) will mean additional expense for China and continued high profits for oil-producing nations supplying China – but rather the volumes involved.

In October 2009, as the world's economies showed signs of recovering from recession more rapidly than forecast, the IEA revised its global oil consumption numbers upwards for both 2009 and 2010. For 2010, global oil demand was revised to 86.1 mn bpd, up by 350,000 bpd over the IEA's previous forecast. The oil-hungry economies of the world will buy and consume this oil and sustained economic recovery will mean that the IEA will probably have to revise its figures upwards once again. Meanwhile the world's oil tanker fleet will continue to be the main mode of transportation. The ships sail on.

Controlling and ensuring an interrupted flow of commodities is not just about controlling territory and land. Supply lines – whether SLOCs or pipelines – also need to be guaranteed, secured and controlled. Protecting the SLOCs from the amorphous and chimera-like threat of piracy or domination by a single shipping fleet controlled by interests perhaps at odds with the client nations is now as important as controlling land. The major economies of the world may not agree on much – they do not agree on how to proceed in Iraq, how to confront the rise of radical Islam in oil-rich countries, how to deal with resurgent nationalism in a petro-dollar economy like Russia's or how to handle the ascendancy of political movements some may not like in countries as various as Venezuela, Burma or Bolivia – but they have agreed and seemingly cooperated so far, to an unprecedented degree, on the need to protect and patrol some of the world's SLOCs.

Notes

Introduction

1   OPEC is a cartel of twelve countries made up of Algeria, Angola, Ecuador, Iran, Iraq, Kuwait, Libya, Nigeria, Qatar, Saudi Arabia, the United Arab Emirates and Venezuela. Ecuador, Gabon and Indonesia were members but have since left the organisation.

2   Statistics and forecasts derived from national governments and the International Energy Agency (IEA).

3   According to the China Association of Automobile Manufacturers (CAAM).

4   Janamitra Devan, Stefano Negri and Jonathan Woetzel, 'Meeting the Challenges of China's Growing Cities', *The McKinsey Quarterly*, 3 (2008).

5   Australia's Cairn Energy started pumping oil from the Rajasthan fields of Mangala, Bhagyam and Aishwarya (MBA) in September 2009. The fields are believed to have a capacity of 30,000 bpd, which will be increased by a further 100,000 bpd in the first half of 2010. Production from Rajasthan could eventually exceed 175,000 bpd. Bill Gammell, non-executive chairman of Cairn India, was quoted as saying, 'We believe there is potential to extend and also enhance peak plateau production from the resource base of the Rajasthan fields above the level of 175,000 bpd.' 'Cairn's Rajasthan Oil Field Ready to Begin Production', *Business Standard* (India), 19 August 2009.

6   The point in time when the maximum rate of global petroleum extraction is reached, after which the rate of production enters terminal decline.

Chapter 1

1   The twenty-eight being Australia, Austria, Belgium, Canada, the Czech Republic, Denmark, Finland, France, Germany, Greece, Hungary, Ireland, Italy, Japan, South Korea, Luxembourg, the Netherlands, New Zealand,

Norway, Poland, Portugal, Slovakia, Spain, Sweden, Switzerland, Turkey, the United Kingdom and the United States.

2 Strategic petroleum reserves data from the IEA, gathered from national statistics.

3 Luke Burgess, 'Has Ghawar Peaked?', *Energy and Capital*, 9 August 2006.

4 Petro-states are defined as oil-rich countries plagued by weak institutions, a poorly functioning public sector, and a high concentration of power and wealth.

5 Lee won the presidential elections in December 2007 with 48.7 per cent of the vote (considered to be a landslide).

Chapter 2

1 'Global Economic Prospects 2007: Managing the Next Wave of Globalisation', *The World Bank*, 1 December 2006.

2 According to the IMF, between 1990 and 2007 Asia's share of global GDP grew from 20.6 per cent to 22.3 per cent while the US share fell from 25.5 per cent to 25.3 per cent and the EU 15's from 30.1 per cent to 28.8 per cent.

3 'World Energy Outlook 2008', *International Energy Agency*, November 2008.

4 Yu Tianyu, 'China Increasingly Reliant on Oil Imports – IEA', *China Daily*, 19 November 2008. The doubling of oil consumption while the dependency ratio does not double is accounted for by the expectation (rather than guarantees) of increased domestic output from Chinese fields.

5 F. Birol, 'World Energy Outlook 2007: China and India Insights', *Council on Foreign Relations*, 27 November 2007.

6 M. Stopford, *Maritime Economics* (London: Routledge, 1997).

7 'Shipbuilding's Changing Guard', *@TheHelm*, Summer 2007.

8 R.W. Tolf, *The Russian Rockefellers: The Saga of the Nobel Family and the Russian Oil Industry* (Palo Alto: Hoover Press, 1976).

9 Iron ore is the primary raw material required for the manufacturing of steel. In 2004 China consumed 39 per cent of the world's traded iron ore and produced only 22 per cent of available ore, according to Merrill Lynch, *Bulk Commodities 101 – Iron Ore*, 18 December 2006.

10 China Shipbuilding and Repairing Industry Report, 2007–2008, *Research in China*, December 2008 (in Chinese).

11 Respectively PetroChina, China National Offshore Oil Co. (CNOOC) and the China Petroleum & Chemical Corporation (Sinopec) and China Ocean Shipping (Group) Company (COSCO), China Shipping and Sinotrans.

12 Mao Shijia quoted in *Seatrade Asia Online*, 27 April 2009.
13 A container being the standard 20 foot, or one 20-foot equivalent unit (TEU).

Chapter 4

1   Quoted in L. Kleveman, *The New Great Game: Blood and Oil in Central Asia* (New York: Atlantic Monthly Press, 2003).
2   Quoted in H. Kissinger, *Diplomacy* (New York: Touchstone, 1994).
3   G. Weaver and A. Mendelson, *America's Mid-life Crisis* (Boston: Intercultural Press, 1983).
4   S. Howarth, *The Fighting Ships of the Rising Sun: The Drama of the Imperial Japanese Navy, 1895–1945* (Springfield, IL: Atheneum, 1983).
5   D. Freeman, *The Straits of Malacca: Gateway or Gauntlet?* (Montreal: McGill-Queen's University Press, 2003).
6   M. Lanteigne, *Chinese Foreign Policy: An Introduction* (London: Routledge, 2009).
7   *China Youth Daily*, 15 June 2004.
8   'Malaysia Calls for Limit on Traffic in Malacca Straits', *Xinhua*, 22 October 2008.
9   *Seatrade Asia Online*, 28 May 2008.
10 Jeremy Page, 'Chinese Billions in Sri Lanka Fund Battle against Tamil Tigers', *The Times*, 2 May 2009.
11 http://www.strategicstudiesinstitute.army.mil/pdffiles/PUB721.pdf.
12 Graham Lees, 'China Seeks Way Around "Malacca Dilemma"', *Myanmar Times*, 20–26 August 2007.
13 S. Michel and M. Beuret, *China Safari: On the Trail of Beijing's Expansion in Africa* (New York: Nation Books, 2009).

Chapter 5

1   Which equals 520 miles or 830 km.
2   'Economic Impact of Piracy in the Gulf of Aden on Global Trade', *US Maritime Administration (MARAD)*, http://www.marad.dot.gov/documents/HOA_Economic Impact of Piracy.pdf.
3   'Reports on Acts of Piracy and Armed Robbery Against Ships (2001–2008)', *International Maritime Organization*, 19 May 2009.
4   Interview with authors.
5   J. Hari, 'You are Being Lied to About Pirates', *The Independent*, 5 January 2009.

6   A semisubmersible heavylift vessel is a ship configured with the majority of its buoyant structure below the water surface and a small cross-sectional area at the water surface. Heavylifts can submerge the majority of their structure, locate beneath another floating vessel, and then de-ballast to pick up the other vessel as cargo.

7   'Somalia Attacks to Top 300', *Lloyd's List*, 9 June 2009.

8   'Annual Piracy Report, 2008', *The ICC International Maritime Bureau (IMB) Piracy Reporting Centre*, released January 2009.

9   D.J. Nincic, 'Maritime Piracy: Implications for Maritime Energy Security', *Journal of Energy Security*, 19 February 2009.

10   Ibid.

11   'China Urges World Navies To Team Up', *Xinhua*, 22 April 2009.

12   Professor Shambaugh's comments on East Asia's SLOCs made during a talk to the Asia Society in New York, *How China's Communist Party Endures*, held on 12 April 2008. See also D. Shambaugh, *China's Military in Transition* (Oxford: Oxford University Press, 1998).

13   'Somali Pirates Hijack Saudi Supertanker', *Oil and Gas Eurasia*, 17 November 2008.

14   'High Cost Keeps Indian Ship Owners to Avoid Ransom Insurance', *ISN Insurance Services Network*, 11 December 2008.

15   'Reports on Acts of Piracy and Armed Robbery Against Ships (2001–2008)', *International Maritime Organization*, 19 May 2009.

Chapter 6

1   International Transports Workers' Federation, *Hebei Spirit* Fact Sheet, 4 December 2008–11 June 2009, http://www.itfglobal.org/campaigns/hebeifacts.cfm.

2   Ibid.

3   Ibid.

4   Ibid.

5   'Treatment of Chawla and Chetan was "Regrettable"', *Lloyd's List*, 25 January 2009.

6   'HKSOA Questions Legality of *Tosa* Crew Detention', *Seatrade Asia Online*, http://www.seatradeasia-online.com/News/4343.html.

7   Ibid.

8   'Indian Sailor Held by Taiwanese Authorities', *The Hindu*, 9 August 2009.

9   Philip Wake, 'Seafarers and Criminalisation', *The Nautical Institute*, http://www.nautinst.org/press/criminalisation.htm.

10   'Nautical Institute's Wake: *Hebei Spirit* verdict is a tragedy for shipping', *Seatrade Asia Online*, 22 December 2008, http://www.seatradeasia-online.com/News/3512.html.

11   Jerry Frank and David Osler, 'Accidents Double on Fleet Boom, Officer Shortage', *Lloyd's List*, 21 February 2008.
12   *Lloyd's List*, 25 June 2009.

Chapter 7

1   James Brooke, 'Landlocked Mongolia's Seafaring Tradition', *New York Times*, 2 July 2004. W. Langewiesche, *The Outlaw Sea: A World of Freedom, Chaos, and Crime* (New York: North Point Press, 2004).
2   International Transport Workers' Federation, 'Flags of Convenience Campaign', ITF Handbook, 13:1.
3   Angelique Chrisafis, 'The Polluter Pays: 30,000 Tonne Oil Disaster Costs French Firm €200m', *The Guardian*, 4 May 2007.
4   Will Hutton, 'Capitalism Must Put Its House in Order', *The Observer*, 24 November 2002.
5   *Lloyd's List*, 7 July 2009.
6   *Fairplay*, 12 October 2000.
7   Jamie Wilson, 'Warning Shot across the Bows Could Signal the End of Corrupt Flags of Convenience', *The Guardian*, 25 June 2002.

Chapter 8

1   Australian Maritime Safety Authority.
2   Shane M. Murphy, Harshit Agrawal, Armin Sorooshian et al., 'Comprehensive Simultaneous Shipboard and Airborne Characterization of Exhaust from a Modern Container Ship at Sea', *Environmental Science & Technology*, 43(13) (2009).
3   The leaked draft of a report from the UN's Intergovernmental Panel on Climate Change (IPCC) was sent to and publicised by the *Guardian* newspaper. See John Vidal, 'True Scale of CO_2 Emissions from Shipping Revealed', *The Guardian*, 13 February 2008.
4   Ibid.
5   Bowring quotes from Matthew Flynn, 'Transport Faces a Green Storm', *Supply Chain Asia*, July/August 2007.
6   Interview with Sam Chambers for *Seatrade*.
7   WWF-UK, Transport and Environment (T&E), Seas At Risk, Friends of the Earth US, Oceana, Clean Air Task Force, Bellona & Stichting de Noordzee Press Release, 'Climate Change Policy on Shipping Continues to Drift. Work Plan Lacks Ambition or a Sense of Urgency', London, 17 July 2009.
8   'ICS and ISF meet in London', *Transport Weekly*, 21 May 2009.
9   Ibid.

10   Neville Smith, 'Maritime Industry Feels the Heat on Global Warming', *Lloyd's List*, 26 April 2009.

11   David Osler, 'Shipping Could Face €4bn Carbon Credit Bill', *Lloyd's List*, 26 October 2009.

12   Sam Chambers, 'Sustainability and the Sea: Asian Shipping – Sustaining World Trade', *Ethical Corporation*, 7 June 2007.

13   Ibid.

14   'International Shipping – Carrier Of World Trade', INTERTANKO press release, 30 November 2006, http://www.intertanko.com/templates/Page.aspx?id=40655.

15   Sam Chambers, 'Sustainability and the Sea: Asian Shipping – Sustaining World Trade', *Ethical Corporation*, 7 June 2007.

16   'Dubai to Host "Green" Shipping Exhibition Next Month', *Thaindian News*, 21 November 2008.

17   Heidi Couch and Alex Morales, 'Solar-Powered Ferries to Sail Hong Kong Harbor, Cut Emissions', *Bloomberg*, 30 July 2009.

18   Ben Webster and Hannah Devlin, 'Cloud Ships on Course to Beat Climate Change, Says Copenhagen Study', *The Times*, 7 August 2009.

Chapter 9

1   'BTC Costs Hit $3.9bn', *Upstream Online*, 19 April 2006.

2   'Russia's Asian Oil Pipeline Costs Soar to $11bn', *Alexander's Gas and Oil Connections*, 14 March 2007.

3   'He Who Pays for the Pipelines Calls the Tune', *The Economist*, 18 July 2009.

4   'China Seeks Closer Ties with Myanmar', *United Press International*, 27 August 2009.

5   Quoted in A. Buncombe, 'China and India are Blamed for Failure of Sanctions on Burma', *The Independent*, 13 August 2009.

6   It is perhaps interesting to note that among the broad swathes of the internet China censors and blocks within the Great Firewall of China, commentary on China's growing role in Burma and relations with the junta are almost totally blocked, indicating the sensitivity Beijing feels around this relationship and its own people's knowledge of it.

7   'SKorea, Russia Discuss Gas Deal Despite Tensions', *Agence France-Presse*, 23 June 2009.

8   JBIC is the international wing of the Japan Finance Corporation, Japan's policy-based financing institution, which has a mandate to fund projects that support Japanese companies overseas.

9   Quoted in John Cherian, 'Engaging Africa', *Frontline*, 25(9), 26 April–9 May 2008.

Index

Index

Index

Index